Got a Problem?
Get a Duck!

GETTING WHERE YOU WANT TO BE

By Arnie Johnson

PUBLISHED BY

EVERGREEN PRESS

1863 Design Drive
Baxter, MN 56425
Phone: (218) 828-6424
www.lakecountryjournal.com

Arnie Johnson began as a lumberjack and an iron miner on northern Minnesota's Iron Range. With the assistance of his wife and business partner, Jo Ann, he went on to build Universal Pensions, Inc.—a nationally recognized retirement-services company.

This is a story of sacrifice, of tenacity, and of one man's commitment to enthusiasm.

"Perhaps one of the reasons for the success of our country can be attributed to the results generated by the true entrepreneur in a free marketplace—for those willing to follow their dreams. Nothing is easy, but coming from nothing except an inherited sense of desire and tenacity, along with a willing and supportive lifetime partner, assured a successful conclusion to Arnie Johnson's dream."
—Al Flaten, former CEO, Nash Finch Corp.

"Arnie and Jo Ann are proof that a young couple, working together and supporting each other, can rise above their surroundings. Their story is an inspiration to anyone willing to take a chance to live their dream."
—Glenn W. Hasse, CEO, Ryt Way Industries

"If anyone doubts that the American dream is alive and well, they should read Arnie's story. The book is a testimony that hard work and tenacity can pay off even if you come from humble beginnings. I recommend it as required reading for our young people as a work of encouragement and opportunity. As a former board member of Universal Pensions, I always enjoyed the culture of the company that Arnie and his team were able to build. Arnie truly cared about his employees.

It's also a love story of two individuals sharing their lives together to accomplish common goals. In today's world of high divorce rates, Arnie and Jo Ann have a formula for a successful relationship. In many growing businesses it's sometimes difficult to balance family and professional life—Arnie and Jo Ann were able to raise a family that remains close and devoted to each other."
—Ron Geiger, President and CEO, Harker's Distribution, Inc.

Got a Problem? Get a Duck!
Getting Where You Want to Be

Evergreen Press of Brainerd Books/December 2001

Printed U.S.A.

ISBN NO: 0-9661599-3-4

Dedication

I dedicate this book to my wife, Jo Ann, and our daughters, Joan and Vicky. For the rest of my life, I hope I can give back to them the part of me they didn't have all the years when I was so dedicated to following my dreams and goals.

TABLE OF CONTENTS

Acknowledgments

Introduction

Acknowledgments

This book would not have been written without the encouragement of employees and friends. They urged me to tell the story of how I started as a lumberjack in the woods, worked in the iron mines on the Iron Range of northern Minnesota, and went on to build a nationally recognized retirement-services company. We pictured it being a small booklet—put together so employees would understand how our company's culture came into being. It didn't take long to see that there was enough material for a book.

I owe a great deal of thanks to Mike Rahn—a writer in the publications area of Universal Pensions, Inc.—for the many hours of hard work and dedication in helping me to write this book. I also thank LAKE COUNTRY JOURNAL MAGAZINE and Evergreen Press who put the final touches on the book. And many years ago, publisher, Chip Borkenhagen, even gave "my duck" a happy face instead of its original frown. I want to recognize Tom Anderson who came to work for me as my controller and grew to become president and COO. Tom was my right hand in building UPI.

To my loving daughters, Joan and Vicky, who grew up during our building years and who learned the true meaning of tenacity early on.

Finally, I want to thank Jo Ann, my wife of forty-three years, who made it possible for me to achieve all my dreams and goals. Without her it would not have happened. She was the support and foundation that held everything together.

Jo Ann, I love you more than you will ever know.

Introduction

This is the story of two people who dreamed of escaping a life in iron handcuffs. We wanted more than just earning enough to get by, while struggling against economic forces and workplace politics over which a miner on northern Minnesota's Iron Range has no control. It's about the dream of a better and independent life—something many dream about but few seriously pursue. It's the story of how my wife, Jo Ann, and I, with no formal education beyond high school, ignored the many reasons why we should choose relative security and accept a fate with limited options and independence. It's a story of overcoming life's limitations with ingenuity, character, will, and especially, enthusiasm.

Jo Ann and I began with no assets other than my modest and sometimes uncertain earnings, first from my trade as a lumberjack in Minnesota's north woods, then as an iron miner. These jobs were supplemented by various part-time jobs to help make ends meet, were followed by a leap-of-faith into insurance and securities sales, and culminated in building a nationally respected retirement-services consulting firm—Universal Pensions, Inc. (UPI).

Despite the material possessions and advantages we lacked, Jo Ann and I had something more important. We had each other and we had determination. We attacked obstacles with tenacity, bent on conquering them together. We discovered that the whole truly is greater than the sum of its parts. Together we were more than two. Together, we found that we were unbeatable.

Our marriage has been a true partnership. While Jo Ann did not officially work with me in establishing and developing UPI, she has always been at my side as a knowledgeable and proven advisor—one I can count on to offer both practical insight and inspired vision. Her contributions helped to shape the success of our company, as well as our life together.

Throughout the years of building Universal Pensions, we shared our ideas and strategies for the business whenever we could. We did so during early-morning "coffeepot sessions" on most Saturdays and Sundays, and during the many evenings, mealtimes, and travel times when we weren't absorbed in the eventful lives of our daughters. (One of my daughters has said that, as a family, "We lived, ate, and breathed business.") Had Jo Ann not been as involved as she was in the entire enterprise, Universal Pensions would probably not have become the industry leader it is.

While we played different roles, Jo Ann and I were pursuing the same dream. This style of life might not appeal to everyone. But I firmly believe there are ways in which people can share themselves and their insights and can provide support to one another, even if their work and their interests put them on different paths.

This book is about our experiences, our strong beliefs, and some of the insights and wisdom we learned along the way. We acquired them as students in the school of hard knocks. It is my hope that this book will prove inspiring and will help others reach their goals and dreams.

Believe in your dreams—pursue them to the point where you can see, touch, smell, and taste them—and approach everything you do with enthusiasm.

PART ONE

"Some people look at things and say, 'Why?'
I dream of things that never were and say,
'Why not?'"

—Paraphrased from George Bernard Shaw's,
Back to Methuselah.

CHAPTER 1

It's Not Where You're From, but Where You're Going

Some people are embarrassed to admit that the road their life has taken has not always been a smooth one. They don't want others to know that they have not always been successful, that their road has led through detours, breakdowns, tough uphill climbs, and dead ends. These proud people don't want to share the fact that they have been down and have experienced failure, or bare-cupboard poverty.

It's not easy to admit to having struggled to make rent or mortgage payments, or having worn threadbare or hand-me-down clothes. Or, in my case, choosing between buying enough groceries for the week or buying a new shirt for an important business meeting.

As much as I have always tried to present an image of success in my business life, I also believe that it's not necessary—or even healthy—to try to hide from or apologize for one's past. I'm not ashamed to admit that I'm from the Iron Range of northern Minnesota where "making do" was as good as it gets for many people. I take pride in where, and what, I've come from.

I wouldn't trade the Jaguar that I'm able to drive today for the oil-guzzling old Ford that I drove forty years ago. I wouldn't voluntarily move from the beautiful lake home where we live back to the trailer home near an open-pit iron mine where Jo Ann and I began raising our family in the 1960s. We lived through extremely tough times, and I now look back and feel a sense of accomplishment and pride in having done so. I don't consider our difficult past something I should hide. Success in life is measured in gains and losses—not always in money, power, or possessions. Success is the distance traveled from a starting point. The more humble the starting point, the more evident is the success.

Achievement and Integrity: Keys to Respect

To have a satisfying life, it's important to have respect. I don't mean the shallow respect we get from others because of the kind of car we drive, the clothes we wear, or the property we own. It's a weakness of human nature, but we often want to be accepted by people we don't even know—people whose judgments should not influence how we live and act. It may be a measure of our insecurity, or perhaps it's a social instinct to fit in and be accepted.

True respect comes from having achieved something that has required hard work, ingenuity, imagination, or some other personal virtue. It does not usually come from being favored by luck, ancestry, or connections. Does anyone really respect a person more because they won a million-dollar lottery jackpot? Do such people really respect themselves? There are many stories of people winning vast sums, then losing this wealth over time, as well as losing spouse, family, and friendships. Success built on luck is often bound to fail, because it brings with it no appreciation of its value, and no formula—typically gained by work and experience—by which to repeat success.

Can respect be earned through marrying or inheriting wealth? I've known people who complain that it's hard to be taken seriously or to be recognized for their accomplishments, because people assume that success was delivered to them on a silver platter.

Integrity is the traveling companion of respect. Without integrity there can be no long-lasting respect. It doesn't take long for our peers, or others around us, to see through the mask of a life built on deception, broken promises, unmet obligations, and a lack of respect for others.

Self-respect is even more important than being respected by others. It's also tougher to earn, because it's easier to deceive others

2

than to deceive ourselves.

Does the value of struggle mean we should give away our possessions, embrace poverty, and make life difficult, just to have something to overcome so we can feel we deserve respect? Probably not, but I can also appreciate the disguised blessing it may be for some people to begin without advantages, to have to learn to rely on themselves.

Tough Times Look Better in the Rear View Mirror

It's easy to be philosophical about struggles when they are in the past. Pain is easier to appreciate when it's behind us. In the rocky times before we achieve success, it's easy to become demoralized. Fortunately, the struggles Jo Ann and I shared did not cause resentment or bitterness between us. When relationships come under the pressures of financial, career, or personal struggles, it's common for people to lash out. Spouses, family members, and others often bear the brunt of such bitterness. Once this becomes a pattern reaction to stress, it's hard to restore trust, acceptance, and faith in the ability to overcome trials together.

In the case of Jo Ann and me, our response to adversity was mutual encouragement and support, and maintaining a positive attitude. Many times we awakened in the middle of the night and spent the remaining hours of darkness talking and working through our obstacles. That's a faithful friend and business partner.

A counselor or psychologist would likely tell us that the most predictable consequences of tough times are resentment, unhappiness, and conflict. For us, the difficulties and our lack of material possessions had the effect of a challenge. Then each accomplishment, each little victory, each small acquisition that bettered our lives, gave us encouragement.

I'm not sure this is something that can be learned, except in the presence of deep and genuine love and respect for one another—love and respect great enough to overpower the urge to blame the other or to let attitudes toward one another be soured. They say that trying times show you who your real friends are. Jo Ann has proven herself to be my best, and most enduring, friend.

Much of the credit can be given to our having been blessed with—or taught—positive attitudes. Witnessing the struggles of people we knew and loved while growing up helped prepare us to endure hardship. We weren't brought up expecting a happily-ever-after married life. Our "we can make it together" spirit gave us the determination not to be stopped in our quest for a better life.

Why Can't We Choose?

Maybe I'm too old-fashioned or optimistic about human nature. But I sometimes wonder why many people seem unable to choose to dedicate themselves to meeting challenges. I know that people have unique personality traits and tendencies—some people may be better prepared for struggle. But I think that too often people say, "I can't," when what they really mean is, "I won't."

I know from experience that the need to budget down to the last dime to make a mortgage payment isn't spirit lifting. No one I know enjoys driving a car with rusted fenders or holes in the muffler. Jo Ann and I had to do these things, and others that were equally humbling.

But there are lessons that can be learned from experiences like this—mainly, that what seem like unbeatable odds, can be beaten. When the forces of life beyond our control leave us ready to throw in the towel, coming out on top only happens if we are willing to push harder and to test ourselves, rather than surrender. I learned this early in life as a wrestler in high school. I might lose a match on a particular night, but there was always another match ahead of me that I knew I had a chance to win. I would sometimes face the same wrestler more than once in a season. If I lost to him the first time, I might learn how to beat him the next.

Giving up guarantees failure. Continuing on at least gives us a chance to come out on top.

Stormy Seas

One of my favorite images comes from sailing—one of my passions in life. No sailor learns how to control a sailing craft by sailing only on calm seas. A sailor builds real skill by facing stormy weather, with waves crashing over the bow, wind blowing strong out of the wrong quarter—defying the elements to make it safely to port, perhaps even to survive.

Character and success are built one wave at a time—learning as we go—until we have mastered enough to know that we almost always have a chance to ride out even the most frightening storm and to come out on top.

I vividly remember the details of struggles that now lie many years behind us. Not all were of a life-or-death variety, but they challenged our resolve and our belief in our ability to cope. While I'm glad those struggles are behind us, they are chapters in our personal history in which I will always take pride. Like pencil marks on a wall to measure how tall a child has grown, our victories, large and small, are marks by which we can measure how much we, too, have grown.

CHAPTER TWO

Hay Bales, Sawdust, Iron, and Grit

The company that Jo Ann and I conceived and built, Universal Pensions, Inc., was founded in 1975 and has grown steadily since that time. At the start of the new millennium, and before my sale of the company in 2001, our employee number had climbed to more than five hundred. It has grown to be respected nationwide for the IRA and pension services it provides to banks, credit unions, insurance companies, brokerage firms, and mutual fund companies in every state of our nation. With saving for retirement viewed as a national priority, now more than ever before, the prospects for its future success are bright.

Running a company that you have built from the ground up can give you a great deal of pleasure. Despite the confidence I had in our management team, I enjoyed staying closely involved right up through the time of the sale of UPI—not in day-to-day operations, but mainly in long-range planning—with Jo Ann's continual support as a sounding board to test my vision and ideas for the future.

The collective spirit and philosophy of a company reflect those who are most involved in running the company on a day-to-day basis. Among the values on which UPI was built is the belief that imagination and persistence will lead you over, around, or through nearly any obstacle. Almost anything can be achieved if we want it badly enough and are willing to work hard to get it.

Beginnings

Our success didn't happen overnight. UPI rose from humble beginnings. I first worked from my home at a desk made from a wooden door, mounted by a hinge to the wall so it could be pulled down when I wanted to work. I eventually graduated to a room in our basement that was dedicated to serving as my office. I realized that to be successful, most businesses need a physical presence in a commercial setting. When sales revenues allowed, I rented office space above a drug store on an upper floor of an aging building in Brainerd's downtown business district. Not as prestigious as Minneapolis's IDS Tower, but it accomplished the purpose of giving more credibility.

From there I moved to a one-room office in a small professional building in west Brainerd. By this time, I actually had one employee! While I had big dreams that someday I would break ground for my own building, in the early days progress was often marked in much smaller steps. At times those steps were so small that it took a sense of humor to appreciate them. Back in the early days of UPI's development, when we referred to our IRA forms department, the department was literally a second shelf that I had added to the office closet! Our space was small, but our dreams were big. With the help of loyal employees who shared our values and dedication, our dreams were fulfilled, despite obstacles and setbacks encountered by nearly every small business.

Family Ties

Values in a company, as in a family, flow from the top down. In a family, the parents and grandparents set the tone for the standards and values of the children. In a company, no matter how good the middle management is, the values of hard work, determination, imagination, and honesty must be present at the top, too. If not, it will be hard to establish them where they must be—at every level in the organization.

Looking back several decades helps to explain the motivation that has driven Jo Ann and me—with great help and dedication from our employees—to accomplish what we have. To a great extent, we are all the products of what we have seen and lived through, what we encountered by accident, and what we were shown. My father, Stanley Johnson, did not make a mark for himself financially. In that sense, he was like most of his fellow miners on the Iron Range. But he was extremely hard working, and he sincerely wanted a better life for his family. The mark he made was in living out his values of dedication and hard work, which made an unforgettable impression on me.

For a couple of years after he and my mother were first married, my dad drove a logging truck for his father's—my grandfather's—logging camp. At that time, the logging camp was a family affair. My mother, Amy, cooked for the lumberjacks and attended to other domestic chores in the camp. She perfected her sewing skills there, skills she later used to help clothe her children when we were growing up.

I doubt that my mother had a complete picture of the opportunities that might lie beyond her immediate surroundings, either when she lived in the seclusion of the north woods logging camp or in the socially and geographically isolated environment of the mining country. But, recalling how she raised us, it's clear to me that she wanted us to be successful in whatever we chose to do and wherever that might lead. To help make that happen, Mother encouraged us to work hard. That was her answer to the question of how to survive when life's opportunities were limited.

She was proud. Part of that pride was shown in wanting us to always be as clean and well dressed as possible. Growing up, I assumed that every youngster wore clothes that his or her mother had made. As I later discovered, store-bought clothes were a luxury, and ours was not a life of luxuries.

When my mother and her brother, Arnold, were growing up in the 1920s, they had very little. Perhaps that's why she was determined to clothe her own family as well as her talents and our limited resources would allow. She told of times when she had only a couple of dresses and her brother only one shirt. These had to be washed almost daily, so they could be worn the next day.

She also missed out on more than just a well-stocked wardrobe when she was growing up. Her mother died of tuberculosis when she was just three years old. As often happened in those days, my mother was boarded out by her father, Forrest Eckert, and she lived with several different families during her early childhood. It would be nine years before my mother would come home to live with her father after he remarried. These events very likely shaped her attitudes about the importance of family and being together.

Holidays were big events, and our family get-togethers often reached clan-gathering proportions. The biggest was usually the Fourth of July, which was spent with aunts, uncles, and cousins at a lake, with a picnic that always included an amazing variety and amount of food. Labor Day was also a time of picnics and family fun, usually with my dad's relatives. It wasn't called Labor Day in Bovey. It was "Farmer's Day," because September was the time of year when vegetable and fruit stands would spring up everywhere. Farmers, as well as others with big gardens, would harvest and sell their produce. There were ribbons for those who had the best produce, and there was great eating for everyone.

Thanksgiving was spent with my mother's side of the family. Turkey, goose, or duck might be the main course, with a supporting cast of mashed potatoes and gravy, sweet potatoes, and mouthwatering desserts. There were delicious sauces and pies— old favorites like apple pie, and wild blueberry and wild raspberry, too.

Christmas was an alternating holiday, celebrated in turn with each parent's side of the family. It was common to have ethnic specialties like Swedish potato sausage, lutefisk, and head cheese (the latter of which I still refuse to touch!). Special meals were a part of every family gathering, no matter what the reason for our being together.

When the men and boys of the family got together to do heavy farm work, like cutting firewood or putting up hay, there would be a special meal, served by the women of the family. We didn't deliberately exclude women and girls from farm work, but more than fifty years ago there were traditions and roles defined by one's gender.

Hard-working Heritage

My father worked almost his entire life as a wage-earning employee. During World War II, he worked in the shipyards in Washington State and later in Pearl Harbor. So that Dad could afford to send his whole paycheck home to support us, he also worked as a waiter on the side. Dad was able to claim at least one direct contribution to the Allied victory. He was part of a crew that did repair work on the radar equipment aboard the battleship *U.S.S. Missouri*, the ship on which the Japanese high command signed the official documents of surrender in August of 1945.

Most of my father's working life was spent employed by big companies in the iron mines of northern Minnesota and in the shipyards of Washington and Hawaii. But he briefly pursued the dream of becoming an independent businessman—the same dream that has motivated me. Not long after World War II, when I was eight years old, we moved from the Iron Range to Sandstone, Minnesota, south of Duluth. There, Dad had discovered and begun the resurrection of a failing, unprofitable gas station. With characteristic Johnson willingness to work hard, he turned it into a thriving business. But Dad wasn't experienced in business matters, and this proved to be his downfall. He hadn't signed a lease with the woman who owned the property. After Dad had gotten the business on its feet and it had become profitable, the owner took the property back and gave it to her son to operate.

Considering how much satisfaction and pride I've had in owning a business, I deeply regret that my father didn't get the chance to live out his dream more fully. Such independence and self-determination—and risk, too—may not be for everyone. But I wish that my father's fate could have been determined more by his wishes than by circumstances beyond his control.

My strongest and most enduring impressions of my dad are of him as an iron miner. Except for brief ventures into other kinds of work, he was a machinist in the mines, as was his father before him. Like many born in northern Minnesota, Dad didn't escape the iron handcuffs of the mines. Despite the rigors of mine work, one demanding job wasn't enough for a man who longed to improve life for his family. When I was in third grade, my parents purchased a small farm in nearby Lawrence Lake, Minnesota, about five miles north of Bovey. Dad would work his shift in the mines, then come home and begin the many farm chores. We raised a few head of beef cattle and hogs, kept some milk cows, as well as chickens for meat and eggs, and harvested vegetables from our garden. These self-supporting pursuits helped to stretch Dad's already-extended paychecks.

Dad worked extremely hard and taught us to do the same. Attending summer camps, killing time at video arcades, or watching television were not part of our culture or generation. At the young ages of eleven and nine, my brother, Jim, and I were working like men, trying to help our struggling family eke out a living.

During the years on the farm, my mother was primarily a housewife. When we arrived home each day, she always had time to listen as we told her about our day at school. Though it was the exception rather than the rule, she occasionally held jobs outside the home. When we lived in California for two years, where Dad was a tool-and-die maker, Mother worked in the Kirkhill Rubber Company factory to help earn money to finance the family's move back to Minnesota.

In dramatic contrast to my family's modest financial means, I had an uncle who was a foreman in the mines. He was a college-educated man who ranked high in the mine's pecking order, with a higher income than ours. His three sons were older than I. They were expected to go to college, and people seemed to have higher expectations for their success than they had for mine. I felt slighted and defensive. As a result, I always felt competitive toward them. I wanted to do well in everything, proving to others that I was their equal, while at the same time, proving it to myself.

My small size was an issue for me, even within my immediate family. I was of a size and physique much like my father; some have said that I was almost his exact image. At five feet six inches, I was half of a Mutt-and-Jeff duo. My younger brother, Jim, was six foot two inches and 220 pounds. We both loved to hunt ducks and do outdoor things with Dad, but Jim was especially passionate about hunting and fishing. I felt that I got more attention than Jim, who was the sometimes-overlooked middle child. But we got along well, unless we happened to be on opposite teams in sports. In hockey, especially, you could count on a scuffle breaking out when we played against each other. Hockey was played on an iced-over creek by our home. We shoveled off a rink, made hockey sticks from tree branches, and used a frozen potato for a puck.

The youngest of the three brothers in our family was Gary, who was six years younger than me, and three and one half years younger than Jim. When he was young, Gary was sickly, though he may have been over-protected. Gary grew out of that and played football in high school. Besides his love of sports, Gary was as passionate about fishing and hunting as Jim. In 1994, Gary died of an untimely heart attack at the young age of 52, leaving behind a daughter, and a family saddened by his death.

For many years, Jim has worked two jobs to give himself and his family the nicer things in life. He is now about to retire from a career working in the natural-gas fields of Wyoming, to come back and settle down in Minnesota and enjoy the fruits of his dedication and hard work.

I looked forward to opportunities to prove myself when the uncles and cousins would gather to do farm work. When we happened to be working on our farm, my dad would give out job assignments. He always gave me the hardest jobs. He felt that when we were working on our own land, our family members should do more of the work than the relatives who helped us, even if I was smaller than my cousins. Like any youngster, I would have liked the easier jobs. But I didn't object because this gave me a chance to show what I could do in front of the cousins.

I sometimes wonder whether being the smallest of the male cousins motivated me to think big—to set goals that some might have thought were out of my league? Did I try to accomplish things that were larger than life because I was smaller than average? Did I fight to earn financial security because life had not handed it to me? I'm not sure of the deep, psychological motivations. I did think big, but I kept those dreams mostly to myself. They were there, beneath the surface, waiting for the right time to be awakened.

CHAPTER THREE

Moving Forward

My relationship with Jo Ann didn't start off with a bang. We were both students at Greenway High School in the town of Coleraine, on Minnesota's Mesabi Iron Range. When Jo Ann was a sophomore and I was a senior, I asked if she would go to the prom with me.

Before the dance, a number of us went to see *Seven Brides for Seven Brothers*, at the Roxie Theater in Coleraine, and afterward went to the dinner hosted by the prom committee at the Bovey Village Hall.

The dance was held in the high school gym, a far cry from some of the ballrooms and country clubs where other students have danced on prom night. We had a live band that played songs like "Rock Around The Clock," "A White Sport Coat," and other tunes recognizable from the classic fifties movie, *American Graffiti*.

After prom, I heard via the grapevine that I hadn't exactly swept Jo Ann off her feet. In fact, "boring" had been used to describe her evening. Apparently, I spent too much time talking about the National Guard, in which I had already enlisted. But while Jo Ann didn't share my enthusiasm for the military, fortunately our prom date didn't put me on her blacklist!

After high school, while I was stationed in Iceland with the United States Army, Jo Ann and I kept in touch by mail. Our letters helped me maintain contact with what was going on back home. Communication was far different from modern e-mail and telephones. A generation ago, long before e-mail, our letters made their way from Iceland to northern Minnesota by airplane, mail truck, and letter carrier. Mail delivery held an element of anticipation.

As our letters continued over the weeks and months, I began to look forward to more than just getting the latest news of our town, the changes going on in the lives of friends, and having a comforting link to life outside the army. I realized that I wanted to be with Jo Ann, and when I came home on my first military leave, we were together almost constantly. (I can still vividly recall the photograph of Jo Ann that I kept in my locker and saw every day.)

Through our letters and during our limited time together, I discovered Jo Ann was adventurous, kind, and sensitive. And she loved to laugh (a virtue appreciated by a practical joker like me). She was also very creative in her interests and in finding enjoyable things to do. She had to be, because I didn't have the finances to court her with dinners, flowers, or gifts.

Our attraction was strengthened by what we had in common. Shared values, priorities, and views of life and the world make a big difference in how well people in any relationship function together, and whether their relationship will endure. While Jo Ann and I have a drive to succeed at everything we do, we also believe deeply in the importance of kindness to others. Over the years, we've spent a great deal of time trying to help others—from men and women seeking business advice, to community development groups and boards of directors. The rewards received from assisting others are often returned as a greater blessing.

Finally back in the states after my tour of duty, I was assigned to Fort Riley, Kansas. I had plenty of time on my hands to think about the many things Jo Ann and I had in common. The more I thought about it, the more certain I was that we could be happy together. When I returned home on leave, I brought an engagement ring. In her parents' living room, I began my proposal by asking Jo Ann to return my high school class ring, which she had been wearing. She was taken by surprise and seemed to be struggling for words. I saw the confusion in her eyes, and—before she could conclude we were breaking up—I smiled, opened the ring box, and slipped the ring on her finger! (She later told me she was shocked and had no idea I would propose.)

Humble Beginnings

The humble expectations that others seemed to have for me certainly looked like they would come true during the period after I was discharged from the U.S. Army. At that time, in 1959, there were no job openings in the iron mines. The G.I. Bill that provided college tuition for some veterans did not apply to discharged enlisted men like me. With no money for further education— even if I had been inclined to pursue it—I had to resort to the same work done by many young, unskilled northern Minnesotans. With my friend Bill Schwartz I cut timber in the forests surrounding Grand Rapids, Bovey, and Coleraine. We joined the throngs of lumberjacks who fed the seemingly endless, wood-gobbling appetites of the paper-making machines at Blandin Paper Company in Grand Rapids.

A chainsaw was the chief tool of my trade. I cut and trimmed timber, which we skidded, loaded, and hauled by truck to Blandin. At the end of a ten-hour day in the woods, I was exhausted. My clothing and face wore a coating of pine-scented sawdust and the less-pleasant aroma of chainsaw exhaust. For all that hard work, I earned from four to six dollars—I once earned eight dollars on a good day.

I learned quickly that any romance linked to a logger's life is only found in fables like those of Paul Bunyan. As for its economic side, my job wasn't one to inspire confidence in a potential bride. Fortunately, Jo Ann had also grown up with the tough economic realities of the Iron Range. Looking past my seemingly poor career prospects, Jo Ann—a person of great faith and determination—said, "Yes." We were married on January 31, 1959. One might have looked at the bleak winter Iron Range landscape on that day—a wickedly cold forty degrees below zero—and imagined this as the view that inspired the phrase, "when hell freezes over."

About one hundred guests attended our wedding in the little white wood-framed church. (The church building had been transplanted from Bovey—where it had once been a Lutheran church— over the rough roads through the iron-ore pits to our community of Lawrence Lake. It was nicknamed, "The Little Church That Could," due to its journey. After the appropriate blessings, it became a Presbyterian church.) Jo Ann and I were the first couple to be married in the newly arrived church, and later our daughters, Joan and Vicky, were the first children to be baptized there.

I wore the suit that had been purchased for my high school graduation, and Jo Ann wore a white dress with a borrowed veil. We had a wedding dance at Forest Lake Lodge in Grand Rapids, but shared the hall with other guests. If you believe it and practice it, love does conquer all. We were about to learn how much we would need to conquer. But we had each other and we were confident that would be enough.

Life on a Shoestring

Following the wedding, we moved into the home we had rented for forty dollars a month. We borrowed furnishings from my cousin Sally—including kitchen chairs, a table, and a refrigerator. Since scrounging has its limits, even for a penniless married couple, we acquired a couch, end tables, and a living room chair for $108 on the payment plan at Sears. It wasn't long, however, before our friends needed their refrigerator back to use in their own home, and we had to find one of our own.

I arranged to purchase a new refrigerator for payments of $10.17 per month, with a verbal commitment to the store's owner that I would work for him to pay off the debt if I were ever unable to make the payment. In this day of easy credit, most people have no idea of how humbling it is to ask, face-to-face, for something so basic—even to the point of promising your servitude to another person. This is one of the reasons why I became committed to reaching financial independence.

All Jo Ann and I owned fit easily into the home we were renting. We had nearly nothing. But that didn't matter, because we didn't know what "something" was. We had grown up in a personal and financial environment in which we saw relatives, friends, acquaintances, and strangers struggling financially their entire lives. We weren't unique. We hadn't been conditioned to believe that the best things of life were rightfully ours. We were used to working hard for what we got.

There's no question that the struggles we faced early in our marriage influenced us. They strengthened us, just as steel tempered by heat becomes stronger. Our struggles prepared us for a future—both personally and in business—neither of us could imagine. It was a future in which we would face situations and choices holding far greater risks, but which we would be prepared to take on with confidence. I wouldn't trade that background of personal struggle for anything. And, aside from the blessing of having parents who led by their examples of hard work and support, I recognize that I was equally blessed to have a spouse who believed in the same things I did—a spouse who felt challenged, not cheated, by our struggles.

Logger to Miner

When the iron mines reopened from their seasonal winter shutdown in the spring following our marriage, I made a job change from lumberjack to miner, having landed a job with the Jones & Laughlin Mining Company in Calumet, Minnesota, ten miles from home. I changed solely for financial reasons. There's little glamour in scrambling around in the bottom of an open-topped ore car, packing straw into the cracks so the chunks of iron ore wouldn't fall out on the journey to the ore docks in Duluth. I worked three different shifts, occupying a very low rung on the ladder of seniority.

One fact of life was the endless battle with red ore dust, which was everywhere, got into everything, and stained one's coveralls to the point of never being truly blue again. Miners had to scrub their skin raw with hot water and generous amounts of soap to get even close to being clean. I'm not sure who looks worse after a day on the job—lumberjacks or iron miners. Neither is a pretty sight.

I made the job change hoping to have a more stable income. We had no idea that even tougher times lay ahead. Soon after I started work in the mines, the United Steel Workers Union went on strike. Along with hundreds of other miners, I was suddenly out of work. The extra benefits eventually received by miners of my level amounted to a few cents per hour. I received no strike benefits and no unemployment pay for the entire 110 days of the strike.

I scrounged for odd jobs, earning money by painting my grandfather's garage, and helping out in Jo Ann's uncle's grocery store. We were lucky enough to be offered a charge account there, to carry us through when the cash flow from odd jobs didn't quite match the grocery bills. To make our situation even more challenging, we became new parents with the birth of our first daughter, Joan, just after the strike ended.

Subsistence Existence

For many people, living in such circumstances would be called poverty. But it was different from what many people experience today, if for no other reason than how people perceived it. We didn't feel we were particularly poor, because nearly everyone around us was in the same situation—struggling to make ends meet. To supplement our groceries, we caught fish, picked wild strawberries and raspberries, and even made chokecherry wine and homemade beer. To earn spending money, we picked wild blueberries and sold them for fifty cents a quart, and harvested wild rice to sell to local processors.

Back then, before the bottom fell out of the wild rice market due to competition from commercial growers, two skilled people in a canoe could make a substantial amount of money picking wild rice. To be equipped to do this, I faced a dilemma. I needed a boat. I purchased an old canvas-covered, cedar-strip canoe for twenty dollars. It was a relic, in very tough shape, and in urgent need of a coat of fiberglass. That posed another problem. We didn't have enough spare cash to buy the fiberglass. I did a mental inventory of possessions I could sell in order to buy the fiberglass to repair the canoe.

I made the emotionally difficult decision to sell my deer rifle—an old, well-worn 38-55 caliber Winchester—that I bought from a neighbor when I was a junior in high school. (I purchased it over the objections of my father, who didn't consider it to be much of a bargain, even with its fifteen-dollar price tag and a free box of shells thrown into the deal.) I sold the rifle for twenty-eight dollars to a man living in Babbitt. I was sure that if the rice harvest was good, Jo Ann and I could make a substantial amount of money. Actually, we probably only made a profit of about one hundred dollars that year.

The rifle had great sentimental value, but sometimes we're forced to overlook sentiment when our financial options are few. About twenty years later, I found the man I had sold it to and asked if he would sell it back. He refused. Perhaps it was because the rifle was old and collectible (or maybe he was just stubborn). Though disappointed, there was nothing I could do but chalk it up as one of life's painful lessons.

At Christmas several years later, I discovered a long, thin, and very heavy package under the tree. When I opened it and saw my old Winchester in the wrappings, I couldn't hold back the tears. Jo Ann paid five hundred dollars for its return. I will always cherish that deer rifle, not just because it was the first I had owned, or that it is a classic, old deer gun, but because its return demonstrated Jo Ann's commitment and kindness. She knew what it meant to me and had the determination to convince the owner to sell it.

One of our staple foods in the early years was venison. This was especially true in the year of our first mining strike. Despite the fact that it was summer, unemployed miners hunted deer to feed their families. Sometimes there were so many of us in the woods we wore red to avoid getting shot. That possibility seemed a greater risk than being arrested for poaching. It was common knowledge that the local game wardens were sympathetic to the miners' financial bind. The wardens were unlikely to go out of their way to catch violators, unless someone complained about a deer being taken out of season. Considering the number of mining families that needed to be fed on the Iron Range during the strike, I wouldn't have wanted to be a visiting hunter in November, coming to that area hoping to find a deer.

Something Better

I was a true son of the Iron Range. I had grown up with friends and family working in the mines at every level, from laborers and foremen, to top-of-the-pay-scale machinists and shovel operators like Jo Ann's father, Fred Bennett. But I couldn't escape the gut feeling that something better was waiting for me outside those mine gates, though I didn't yet know what it might be.

The first opportunity to test this conviction came as an offer to become a partner in an excavating business that was being started by my friend and former logging partner, Bill Schwartz. This meant abandoning the comforting certainty of being paid a predictable number of dollars for a given number of hours worked, and other benefits of working for a large employer. Not everyone is willing to take this kind of risk. But, lured by the hope of independence, Jo Ann and I were daring enough to try. I turned in my resignation at the mine.

You can't run an excavating company without a dump truck, so I traded in our only car as a down payment on a truck. The dump truck became our family vehicle. On grocery day, Jo Ann never had any trouble finding our vehicle in the parking lot. Most wives would be mortified to ride to the grocery store in a dump truck, but if Jo Ann was embarrassed, she hid it well, probably to protect my pride.

But all that glittered was not golden. Considering all the statistics our government keeps, I'm sure that in some agency there is a person who records how many new businesses fail. From what I've learned over a lifetime of seeking self-employment and watching many new business start-ups, I would conclude that most new ventures fail. It wasn't long before our attempt also seemed headed for the statistical graveyard. The typical problems of cash flow, making payments on equipment, coaxing payments from customers, and dealing with other headaches, were even straining the friendship that brought Bill and me together.

For the sake of our friendship and my family's financial well being, I decided to leave our excavating venture, so Bill could try to make it on his own. The dump truck, which for me had symbolized the excitement and opportunity of being an entrepreneur, went back to the dealer in Grand Rapids where I had purchased it. My first real effort in business had been a failure. I was forced to retreat to the security of the iron mines.

There was another penalty for my business failure, too. Having given up my job in a local mine, the only job now available required us to move to Babbitt—one hundred miles northeast. The mining companies there were extracting a new, and once-unprofitable, iron ore called taconite. We bought a home in a company-housing tract with no money down. For transportation, I bought a much-used 1953 Ford two-door sedan that burned a quart of oil every 150 miles!

Up the Mine Ladder

I began working as a general laborer. Several sets of ore-stained coveralls later, I moved up the job ladder to Cat skinner—driving one of the D-8 Caterpillar bulldozers used to scrape and smooth the network of roads to the excavation sites within the pit. I then became a truck driver, guiding one of the mine's huge, ninety-ton ore trucks along the dust-choked roads in and out of the open pits.

I was a perfectionist. Though some people might consider road building mundane and uncreative, I tried to put whatever excellence I could into the job. I studied how roads should be built, and did my best to bank or elevate the turns properly. My efforts to achieve perfection weren't shared by everyone. I still remember my frustration when I came to work the next day to find that an operator on the shift before mine—who obviously didn't understand good road building—had carelessly undone my painstaking banking and grading. In the iron mines, like everywhere, the pursuit of excellence can be a thankless, uphill battle.

I might have been one of the few foolish enough to pursue excellence in that work environment. Some people work hard and do their best no matter what their job. Others take advantage of opportunities not to perform. I saw this too often and was discouraged by it. One worker bragged that he only used up one welding rod during his entire eight-hour shift. Things like this made me want to leave a work environment where merit was not the path to job advancement.

Maybe I'm old fashioned. But seeing fellow workers acting proud of under-performance was hard to stomach. At key times in our country, the contributions of unions have been great; for example, unions have helped American workers escape dangerous and unfair working conditions. But one of the consequences of too much job security is that people who are unmotivated can take their unproductive attitudes to extremes. When this happens, it undermines morale and the performance of other workers, reduces a company's productivity, and makes that company—or perhaps an entire industry—uncompetitive in the world marketplace. This was another reason I felt a growing need to find another way to make a living.

CHAPTER FOUR

Whatever It Takes

Many people mistakenly believe that every employee in a highly unionized industry such as mining is paid well enough to be comfortable. This simply wasn't so, especially at the low seniority and classification levels where I was employed during my early years as a miner. Whenever the miners were able to save a little money and get ahead, another labor strike would be called, and they were out of work again. In order to afford life's little luxuries, to enjoy hobbies, or have anything beyond the basics, I took on second and third jobs.

For one season, one of these sidelines was working on a sod farm. If you've ever laid a few rolls of sod in your own yard, you know how dirty a job it is. In the heat of midsummer, sweat turns the dirt accumulating on your arms, neck, and face to black mud. By day's end, it was hard to tell whether there was more dirt on me or on the rolls of sod.

My daily routine was to work the 11 p.m. to 7 a.m. shift driving trucks in the mine, get home at about 7:30 in the morning, eat a big breakfast, then head for the sod fields to work a full day. I would arrive home in time for dinner, get as much sleep as I could, and be back at the mine for the 11 p.m. start of my next shift. It was probably a good thing that the sod-growing season is short on the Iron Range.

During the school year, I also drove a schoolbus. Bus driving was cleaner work than handling sod, but I can't say it was necessarily good for my sanity. Based on my tour of hazardous duty as a bus driver, I have endless respect for drivers who are able to maintain control over both themselves and the kids. I also sold archery equipment out of my home. My favorite hobby became a means to make extra money for some of life's small luxuries.

Jo Ann and I were not willing to settle for having only those rewards that an eight-hour workday as a miner could provide. We didn't abandon our dreams and unquestioningly accept the limitations of a miner's income. We looked at the things in life we wanted, and then we looked for extra income opportunities to make them happen. Jo Ann could have taken a job outside our home instead of my taking second or third jobs. But we chose that she would devote her time to our home and family, while I concentrated on producing income. Our choice might not be right for everyone, but it worked for us.

Fortune or Fate?

People say, "Things happen for a reason." Whether or not you believe that, the events of life often work out so neatly that it seems as if a particular thing was meant to be. Jo Ann and I had been discussing what our future would hold if I kept working in the mines, and what we might have to do to make a break from it. For now, the mortgage payments on our home bound us tightly to my job in the mines. Without such a large mortgage, Jo Ann and I would be free to look at job options and different locations, if that became necessary.

We hadn't shared any of our thoughts of relocating with anyone. That made it all the more surprising when a recently hired employee asked me—out of the blue—if we'd consider selling our home.

It didn't take us long to decide. We packed up our belongings—which didn't amount to much—and moved into a 10 x 46-foot mobile home we had purchased. We discovered that being flexible in our housing, meant a trade-off in how we lived, too. Space and comfort were the biggest losses. Our living room had a hinged wall that swung out of the way to allow a three-quarter-size bed to drop down for sleeping. This was our master bedroom.

"Cozy" is fine for a vacation at the lake, but it's not as acceptable when it's merely another way of saying "small." Our quarters were likely to remain small for the foreseeable future. The only real bedroom in our trailer was where Joan and our recently arrived second daughter, Vicky, slept. In those tight quarters, we would have had no need for the modern baby monitors today's parents use to keep track of their little ones.

Fate Makes an Offer

My friend, Dick Charlton, knew I was looking for a way out of the mines. His father had an insurance agency covering much of northeastern Minnesota and he had offered his son a chance to sell insurance part time. Dick put in a word for me. It wasn't long before his father offered me an opportunity as well.

All I knew about insurance was that it was one of life's necessary evils, and that Dick's dad earned a pretty comfortable living from it. Since it would only be part time, I could get my feet wet, learn the business, and keep the security of my mining job. I hoped that selling insurance would be my big chance.

I saw the insurance business as a possible ticket to independence, and a chance to be rewarded in proportion to my willingness to learn and work hard. Accepting the offer was the easy part. I soon found myself studying hard for the insurance license exam. Having failed once in an attempt at independence, I was afraid to let this chance slip through my fingers.

I nearly wore out the study guides preparing for the test. I was extremely proud to earn a perfect 100 percent on the test. In spite of never having made a sales presentation, let alone sold an insurance policy, I was filled with confidence that I could measure up to the challenge.

Perhaps it was because I was still tied to my job in the mines, but it wasn't long before the glow of the 100-percent score began to dim, as I faced the grind of actually doing the work. At times, it seemed as though I had merely traded my old part-time jobs for one that allowed me to dress better. It took a lot of time to prepare for and make my sales presentations.

My real hope was that by learning the business, I'd get my foot in a door that would eventually lead to a new career. At the time, I was working a lot of swing shifts in the mine—a different shift from week to week. I generally worked weekends, with two days off during the week. Some days my mind seemed to be in two worlds at the same time. As I steered my ninety-ton ore truck along mine pit roads, my mind might be off somewhere else entirely, doing mental dry runs to refine my sales presentations. Fortunately, I never totally forgot where I was and what I was doing, or I might have put my ore truck in the ditch or over an embankment.

On my two days off from the mines each week, I sold insurance. The biggest obstacle I faced was that I couldn't sell near where Jo Ann and I lived, in places where I had friends and other personal contacts that might have made those first sales easier. To avoid competing with the friend who had helped get me into the business, I had a different sales territory. Before I could make any presentations I had to drive seventy-five winding, wooded miles from Babbitt to the North Shore of Lake Superior.

For some people, this long-distance commute might have been too great to seem worth it. But I knew that I was now taking small first steps on a path that might lead to what I wanted more than almost anything: personal and financial independence. I could handle putting a few more miles on my car, losing a little more sleep, consuming a few more Thermos bottles full of coffee and dodging a few more deer and moose on that lonely highway that led to my territory. I had been given a chance, and I intended to make the most of it.

It wasn't long before I made a few sales. I felt certain that, sooner or later, I would be asked to consider leaving the mines to sell insurance full time. Even though I expected it, when the chance came, I hesitated. I had put so much effort into preparing myself to sell insurance, yet I flinched. Why? Having quit the mines once before, only to retreat there for security when my contracting venture went sour, had made me gun shy. Would I fail again?

Then my sales manager asked me a simple question, but one that would change my life forever—by changing the way I approached difficult decisions.

"If you go into insurance sales full time, and don't make it, what's the worst thing that's likely to happen?"

"I might have to go back to the mines," I replied. Regardless of the sense of failure and embarrassment I would experience if this happened—I knew I would be no worse off than I was now. More importantly, instinct told me that if I backed away from this challenge, I might never have the courage to try again. From this crossroads, I learned that if we fail to challenge ourselves, fail to step up when our best effort is needed, our self-esteem begins to waver. We condition ourselves to retreat instead of moving forward with confidence. We may be able to ignore what others say, but it's much harder to ignore the inner voice that reminds us of our weakness and lack of faith.

Going For It

By now I had achieved enough success in selling insurance to feel that I might be able to make it. I had earned two weeks of paid vacation from the mines, so I made a proposal to my insurance manager. "Work with me full time for one week during my vacation, and I'll work the second week alone. At the end of that time, if I think I can earn enough, I'll quit the mines and go full time."

He agreed and promised to spend a week helping me. I was extremely disappointed when, having worked with me for just three days—days when we didn't make a single sale—my manager told me he had other commitments and left me on my own.

I don't know whether this was his way of putting me to the test, but I was upset that he backed out. After all, I was deciding whether I would put it all on the line and risk everything on this new job. But I kept at it, making sales presentations on my own for the next week and a half, but still no sales. If I was looking for an excuse to stay with my job in the mine, I certainly had one. Yet, somehow, lacking any reasonable explanation for my optimism, I was confident that I could do the job and be a success at it.

The day I went back to the mine after my two weeks of working vacation, everything seemed slightly different. Even before I officially gave my notice, I felt a detachment, a strange sense of being part employee and part visitor. It was odd knowing that, within mere days, I would not be part of the crew. I would not be sharing their jokes, the talk of wives and kids, of fishing or deer hunting, or how our union would do in the next round of bargaining.

The background buzz of mingling voices, the noise of machinery—sounds that on other days I was unconscious of—stood out with a clarity I had never remembered. The seriousness of the day's decision put all my senses on full alert. I was both exhilarated and scared out of my wits. I was taking not only my own life in my hands, but the lives of those dear to me as well. It would have been a good time to lose my nerve, but I didn't.

I repeated to myself the question asked by my manager. "What is the worst thing that can happen?" Comforted by the answer, "We will survive," I gave my notice. It was accepted with raised eyebrows and, "He'll be back," murmurs from my fellow miners. Two weeks later, I was on my own.

I had traded a secure job with a modest but guaranteed income, for a high-burnout-rate job that offered no guarantees and no paid expenses, only sales commissions. It was unquestionably a risk. But the world is full of people who are afraid to take risks. I don't encourage irresponsibility, but I admire the person who has a dream and is willing to wrestle with risk to try to make that dream come true.

To be closer to my new sales territory, we moved our trailer home from Babbitt to Taconite, a tiny community of 137 people not far from where Jo Ann and I grew up in Itasca County. I felt both great freedom and great fear. I was my own boss, but I had given up our family's safety net. Regardless of what human-resources experts say about fear as being a poor personnel management tactic, fear was a great motivator for me.

I knew that the wolf would soon be howling at our door if I

didn't produce, so I threw my energies into my new career. I put in long hours, racking up thousands of miles to make sales presentations and visit clients. Even though I had finished in the bottom half of my graduating class of ninety-seven students at Greenway High School, I became a student again. I enrolled in insurance-underwriting classes, traveling eighty-five miles each way to Duluth to attend. I studied as hard as my selling time would allow in order to master the products I wanted to offer my customers and prospects. One of these products was retirement plans, which—though I couldn't have known it at the time—would one day be the core of the company I would establish.

Within two years I rose from the status of rookie insurance agent to the top of the company's regional sales force. My next advancement was to the position of general agent, and—not long after—regional director. Having reached this professional milepost, it became clear that a new world of possibilities lay before us, limited only by our imagination and determination.

Dare to Try

Jo Ann and I found an uncharted road and dared to take it. It was a road with possibilities and pitfalls we couldn't begin to imagine. Somehow, our instincts and our early experiences gave us the courage to risk what little we had. We dared to try, knowing that the worst that might happen was that we might not succeed. We might have to regroup and try again. Above all, we came to understand that we would only fail if we gave up on our dream and quit trying.

From the **Family** *Album*

STAN AND AMY JOHNSON,
GARY, JIM, AND ARNOLD.

YOUNG ARNOLD AT HOME.

THE JOHNSON BROTHERS:
ARNOLD, JIM, AND GARY.

CATCHER ARNIE PLAYING BASEBALL.

ARNIE'S MOTHER'S FAMILY—THE ECKERTS.
ARNIE IS AT FAR RIGHT.

ARNIE AND HIS FATHER-IN-LAW, FRED BENNETT.

HIGH SCHOOL GRADUATION—
CLASS OF 1956.

SENIOR ARNIE AND SOPHOMORE
JO ANN ATTEND PROM.

Mr. and Mrs. Arnie and Jo Ann Johnson—January 31, 1959.

Lawron
Presbyterian
Church where
Arnie and Jo Ann
were wed.

ARNIE'S FIRST DEER
TAKEN WITH A BOW
AND ARROW.

ARNOLD ON DUTY IN ICELAND.

ARNIE AT AN ARMY BASE.

ARNIE'S
FIRST VEHICLE.

HOME IN BABBITT FOR EIGHT MONTHS.

Joan and Vicky with Easter baskets.

Arnie reunited with his prized rifle.

Unloading at Blandin Paper Company.

ARNIE IN HIS OFFICE
AT THE CORPORATE HEADQUARTERS OF UNIVERSAL PENSIONS, INC.

CHAPTER FIVE

One Plus One Is Greater Than Two

(The following describes our feelings about the importance of strong, supportive relationships in reaching goals in life. These thoughts are expressed first from my viewpoint, then Jo Ann's.)

Together We're Strong

I'm sure you've heard the expression, "the whole is greater than the sum of the parts." By combining two or more ingredients, or people, or chemicals, or what-have-you, the results you get may be more than you would expect from the combination of those elements. This is how I would describe the relationship I have had with Jo Ann for more than four decades.

Examples are found everywhere in life. One of the most obvious is a successful sports team. Relationships and combined skills sometimes result in a team being able to accomplish more than you would have expected from their individual players. It's sometimes referred to as, "playing over their heads."

One memorable example was the U.S. men's hockey team that competed for the gold medal in the 1980 Winter Olympics at Lake Placid, New York. This team had a lot of talent, especially when you consider that almost all its members were college students. But few, if any, hockey experts at the time thought this collection of youngsters would be a match for some of the European teams— many of whose players were older, seasoned by greater experience, or had played professionally. (This was long before it became accepted practice for hockey professionals to compete in the Olympics.)

Their most intimidating opponent was the Russian hockey team. Most of its members were full-time players—military personnel whose only real assignment was to play hockey and bring acclaim to the Soviet Union. They played hockey with military precision, too. This was proven year after year both in international competition and exhibitions in which they defeated teams made up of many of the best professionals from the National Hockey League.

What the U.S. hockey team lacked in maturity and experience, it made up for in chemistry and youthful optimism. More than just individual players who could skate, shoot, and handle a puck, the players were willing to be coached, and Coach Herb Brooks was an inspiring leader. They believed him when he said, "You were born to be players. You were meant to be here." These young men were playing for both personal and national pride. They had been coached to believe they had a date with destiny.

Even the least sports-minded person heard about the U.S. team winning the gold medal that year. Millions witnessed the power of belief in one's self, and an unwillingness to be beaten. They saw a chemistry that made it possible for the young team to overcome the Russians' experience and superior talent. The world watched as the cool, methodical, greatly feared Russian team came unglued when faced with a collective will to win that was superior to talent alone.

This kind of chemistry also sometimes develops within a business, allowing it to achieve breakthroughs and growth that other companies—some of which appear to have equal or greater talent—have a hard time pulling off. Apple Computer was that kind of company during the formative period of the home-computing age. I believe Universal Pensions had that kind of chemistry—allowing us to grow from only two people in a one-room office, to more than five hundred people serving the nation's most successful financial organizations.

Genuine Teamwork

On a personal level, I also believe the "team principle" of combined energies and skills has a lot to do with the success experienced by Jo Ann and me. We each have our own strengths and special talents. When combined, they've enabled us to work together to grow a successful company, as well as a successful marriage and family. People are more effective when they work together, and do not try to live, work, and create by themselves.

Some people try to accomplish things by themselves—ignoring others who could help them, often those right in their midst. Even when these people accomplish something significant, they could probably have accomplished more, or achieved it more easily, if they had had a partner or team relationship.

Within our partnership, our career paths could not have been more different. While I often worked two or three jobs, Jo Ann has been a homemaker for our entire marriage. I was the only outside-the-home worker because that was the direction in which our mutual preferences led us. I did not resent the fact that Jo Ann didn't earn income from a job outside our home. She, in turn, did not resent that I wasn't able to share the domestic responsibilities, nor that I wasn't a highly paid, up-and-coming executive who could have made our early years of marriage easier.

In any relationship where there are tasks—whether at home or in the professional world—there must be an understanding of individual responsibilities. Some are shared and some are not. The arrangement that worked for us might be different from the division of responsibilities preferred by others. But most importantly, these expectations were mutual. When they're not, a personal relationship is like a football team with its signals crossed. Instead of putting points on the board, the team fumbles, misses opportunities, and eventually loses the game.

Unlike some women in the role of traditional housewife, Jo Ann was also a true participant in financial matters beyond the household budget. She was involved in the decisions to make the job changes I made—as well as many of the decisions that affected the building of Universal Pensions. In the early years of our marriage, it was Jo Ann's encouragement, calm reasoning, and confidence that helped me to take a leap of faith and leave the mines, not once, but twice, even though my first attempt ended in failure.

As Universal Pensions was growing from its one-room rented

office—a new company that only a few small-town bankers had heard of—and becoming a highly respected consulting firm, I always sought her advice and instinctive good judgment. I did so when deciding such issues as new marketing ideas, the company's expansion, hiring key employees, and other issues on which the future of the business hinged. Jo Ann critiqued my ideas, played devil's advocate, and often raised issues and suggested directions I had not thought of. Her instincts about people are exceptional and have usually been right on target. (She said, "Yes," to my proposal of marriage, didn't she?) The importance of Jo Ann's lifelong input has been incalculable. We shared many of the decisions, and certainly the struggles, to make our pension-consulting business a success. We now share a very good life, which has come as a payoff for the sacrifices we made for so many years. And there were big sacrifices, especially in the days after I had left the mines to try to find financial independence.

Resourcefulness

Many people today expect to be taken care of. Or, they expect the good things in life to come easily. Many believe that "the good life" is a right, rather than an achievement. We didn't. And, at those rare times when something was given to us, we were uncomfortable. When our daughter, Joan, was born, and my parents discovered that we were buying five dollars worth of heating oil at a time because we couldn't afford more, they gave us fifty dollars to fill our tank. Because we hated to be in someone's debt, we repaid them within a few months. Jo Ann's father, Fred, taught me to keep a ten dollar bill tucked away in my wallet—separate from the other money. Before UPI, when I was on commission, it was the emergency grocery money. If I needed to use it, I "paid it back," as soon as possible.

Jo Ann and I made the best of what we had. We were forced to try creative ways to cut corners and stretch our meager income. At a time when our grocery budget was tight, we sometimes ate potato soup for a week. Venison was a common menu item (sometimes both in and out of season). Jo Ann learned so many different ways to fix venison she could probably write a gourmet venison cookbook.

Because we didn't have a sausage stuffer, we once came up with a creative way to make potato sausage—a family Christmas tradition. We removed the ends from an old, hollow plastic rolling pin (which had been a wedding gift) to make a cylinder, stretched the sausage casing over one end, and used a broom handle covered with a plastic bag to force the sausage contents into the casing from the other end.

Rather than be stopped by what seemed like an impossible obstacle, we came up with a creative solution. I'm not sure whether the sausage tasted great because it actually was better, or because we had to be resourceful in making it. What should have been a two-hour job took us eight hours, but it seemed worth it. We still make potato sausage today at Christmas, as much as sixty to seventy-five pounds, some of which we give to others. And, though we don't use it for sausage, Jo Ann still uses that rolling pin to roll out pie crusts.

"Creative getting by" was an everyday necessity. Jo Ann had an amazing ability to improvise. Once, when she wanted a place to store our bathroom towels, she used a wooden box in which I had shipped my clothing back from Iceland when my tour of duty ended. She hung a piece of plastic on a rawhide shoelace to serve as a curtain to hide the towels. In the early years of our marriage, Jo Ann washed our daughters' cloth diapers and outfits on a washboard, rubbing her knuckles raw to get the clothes clean. She hung the laundry outside to dry, even in winter. When the laundry froze, she took it inside to thaw and finish drying.

We wanted to improve our home, even if it was only a trailer. We tried to put away a dollar here or there to make improvements. Sometimes it was no more than buying a board or two to build something. We dug up trees and shrubs in the woods and planted them in the yard. We improved our way of life—often one tiny step at a time.

The curtains and attempts at landscaping weren't the most valuable things we received from our efforts. More valuable was the reinforcement we felt after struggling for something and finding a way to get it, even though it might be small. This proved that we could find a path to what we wanted, even if it was slow and diffi-cult. There were ways to reach a brighter future, with imagination, positive thinking, and hard work.

Appreciating Our Roots

Today I have the luxury of not worrying about basic expenses, and can indulge myself in extras, like outfitting a home workshop with first-class woodworking tools and power equipment. But the appreciation I have for these things is nowhere near the apprecia-tion I had in the old days for the simple things we saved and sac-rificed for.

When I look back at how we lived—in mining company housing or a trailer home without a proper bedroom; eating fish, venison, and food from the land; going without the simple fringe benefits people today take for granted—I'm amazed that we didn't lose hope. I'm amazed we had enough faith in the future to tough it out.

My only explanation is that we have always been the kind of enthusiastic people who can think positively, who can shut out negatives, and not let them weigh us down to the point of discour-agement or despair. Jo Ann and I have always had similar goals and beliefs. We've been able to select goals and commit ourselves to reaching them, no matter what the obstacles. Not everyone can say that; or, perhaps, not everyone is willing to be that committed to a cause.

Communication has been one of the most powerful weapons in our search for success and a better life. Throughout our four decades of marriage, Jo Ann and I have always talked openly with one another about our dreams for the future. Fortunately, our dreams have been similar. We also have had great faith in our-selves and in one another. We instinctively believed that if we refused to give up, we would be rewarded with success in the end.

With the time I've had to spend away from home on business, time together was usually at a premium. But when we were together, Jo Ann and I had the capacity, and just as importantly the desire, to communicate.

Communication isn't easy. But without it, whether in your profession or in your home and personal life, it's almost impossible for two or more people to effectively work together to reach objectives, let alone exist together happily. There is no mysterious, fail-safe formula for successful communication. It takes a genuine belief in the importance of communication, and an unwavering commitment to ensuring that constant, open, goal-oriented communication will take place.

That was our secret weapon. With shared values and determination, it can work for almost anyone.

In Her Own Words

(The following are personal reflections of my wife, Jo Ann Johnson.)

Life was very different more than forty years ago when Arnie and I were first married. We never considered giving up and walking away from a problem to be an option. We didn't expect to be taken care of by others, which some people so easily fall back on today. Divorce, bankruptcy, or welfare were also not options or even considered as possibilities. Arnie and I entered married life knowing that it would be a struggle. We didn't start out with the attitude that someone would be around to bail us out if things got difficult.

We knew we had to rely on each other. When one of us felt discouraged and unsure of what our next step should be, we talked about our options until we could make a decision. Whatever it might be, with us it would definitely be some kind of step. We didn't believe in standing still, but in moving in one direction or another. This philosophy is expressed so well by playwright George Bernard Shaw: "People are always blaming circumstances for what they are. I don't believe in circumstances. The people who get on in life look for the circumstances they want; and if they can't find them, make them."

For us, it was a matter of either accepting the circumstances we had or making changes to those circumstances. To accept the idea that—whatever the circumstances we faced—we had no power to change them, was not in our makeup or view of life. Many people we knew faced similar difficult financial situations. But I think what made us different was having very well-defined priorities and great motivation. We wanted to make a major change in our lives more than most people we knew.

A nicer, larger home for our family, a car that wasn't rusted and burning oil, and enough money so we didn't have to worry about stretching our groceries to make them last from paycheck to paycheck—these were dreams that we turned into goals. I have always supported Arnie in his belief that when you're pursuing something you want very badly, you have to focus on it and imagine it to the point where you can almost detect it with your senses—you can almost taste, smell, or feel it. It sounds almost mystical, but we see this as part of the process by which our desires first became dreams, and then goals, which we then pursued with the knowledge that we could reach them.

Homemade and Homegrown

Our work ethic didn't come from motivational books, tapes, or speakers, but from the example of our parents. Their personal struggles and self-denial were our inspiration. I'll never forget my father once telling me of making his own winter shoes, using rubber cut from old inner tubes. When sacrifices like this involve people close to you, you admire their courage, and you realize that obstacles of almost any size can be overcome.

I learned I was capable of making similar sacrifices. Because money was scarce in the early years of our marriage, I used my imagination to make our limited resources go farther. I became a creative cook. I found I could make a half-pound of hamburger and two polish sausages last for a week. I would take a quarter pound of hamburger—usually venison burger—add slices of Polish sausage, brown it, and make a gravy.

We usually mixed home-canned green beans, corn, or carrots with potatoes we got from my parents. Dad proudly loaded us up with homegrown fruits and vegetables. It was his own special gift. We made a little meat go a very long way. We probably ate potatoes and gravy far more often than anyone would want to today. From time to time, we had a special treat—like when my parents would give us canned blueberries and raspberries.

For another cost-cutting meal, I would pound a venison steak to tenderize and flatten it, cover it with flour, fry it in a pan, and cover it with tomatoes. Or I prepared venison chops with gravy. Today, a family might have venison or other wild game occasionally, but venison was our staple meat—steaks, roasts, chops, and venison burger were always on the menu. We used beef or other meat from the butcher or the grocery store when we had to, to supplement the venison, rather than the other way around. We even butchered the deer ourselves.

There were many other ways to economize. For a long time, I made do with one pair of shoes for every occasion. A couple of pairs of underwear, washed out every other day by hand, were sufficient. Extra money for gas to go driving or to go to the movies was often not there. We entertained ourselves with inexpensive pastimes, like playing cards—whist was one of our favorites.

Fun on a Budget

When we had been married for four or five years, we took our girls camping, which became a frequent family activity. We both enjoyed the outdoors, and camping was inexpensive. Where we camped, there was no campground fee. We brought food from home and added fish that we caught. We gathered our own wood. Considering how much fun we had, it was an amazing bargain.

We stretched our budget to get our camping gear. We saved Gold Bond Stamps and S & H Green Stamps that came with groceries, and when we had filled enough books, we redeemed them for sleeping bags, cookware, and a Coleman stove and lantern. Our first tent was a small, much-used tent that someone we knew had discarded—we had to spread a raincoat over its doorway when it rained! But it served its purpose, and we weren't too proud to make the most of it.

Because money was scarce, we planned ahead. In order to afford our summer camping trips, we started putting away some of the essentials months before. When there was enough money after bills were paid out of Arnie's paycheck, we might buy canned food, fruit, or vegetables for the camping trip that was still months away. It might seem ridiculously thrifty, but it was the one way we could be sure we would have all the essentials for the trips that were such an important part of our family life.

Arnie and I might seem fanatical in our stubbornness to take care of ourselves. But it wasn't our style to turn to others for help. Most people we knew would, themselves, have been stretched to be able to help us. We rarely let on, even to our parents, how hard things were at times. Later, when we did share some of our struggles with them, they were shocked. Once when Arnie and I were returning home from a visit with my parents, we had only fifty cents between the two of us. We had the two girls in our old car and one hundred miles to go. Our gas line froze, and we had to write a check for fifty cents, with only a dollar and a half in our checking account, and several days to go before payday.

Other incidents are humorous. On our third anniversary, I was pregnant with our second child, Vicky. We were very low on cash, and I was craving tomatoes and cucumbers. I'm probably the only woman ever to be given tomatoes and cucumbers as an anniversary gift.

I didn't have real maternity clothes during my first pregnancy. I held my old slacks together with a huge safety pin where they gapped open at the waist. My maternity tops? Arnie's shirts. When I went to the doctor's office for my first prenatal appointment, I borrowed an outfit from a thoughtful cousin. Later, wanting me to feel good about how I looked for my baby shower, my mom bought me an outfit at a local store.

Life without the simple comforts, struggling to provide basic needs, is difficult any time. But when you're pregnant—often feeling unattractive, wanting the best for the child you're about to bring into the world—remaining positive and hopeful is an even bigger challenge. But the alternative to hope is despair, and that was something we always found a way to rise above.

Our babies never wore Pampers. Funds were too scarce to be wasted on disposable diapers. Both daughters wore cloth diapers, washed out daily on a scrub board in a washtub for our firstborn, Joan, and in a washing machine by the time we had our second child, Vicky.

In the early days our cars were never new, or even dependable. When Arnie was still working in the mines, on cold winter nights he often went outside several times to start the car, to make sure it would start in the morning so he could make it to work. During the year we lived in the Minneapolis area (Arnie was selling insurance), we could only afford one car. I didn't learn to drive until six years after we were married.

Joan and Vicky were in the second and first grades, and I routinely walked a mile to their school to help with class field trips or Campfire Girl activities. The girls and I also walked home that long distance together. With Arnie on the road, many times for an entire week, we walked to the grocery store whenever we ran out of necessities.

Built on Trust

I had great faith in Arnie. I trusted that he would find a way to support us, because he knew how to work hard and he had a strong drive to succeed. He dreamed and planned on someday having the things that we wanted—much more than we were used to. That doesn't mean we were never discouraged. I remember times when Arnie was selling insurance and sales were not going his way. I would try to spark his enthusiasm by encouraging him to try a new strategy or a new presentation.

I listened to him over and over, offering my views and suggestions for changes. Sooner or later we would succeed in relighting the fire of enthusiasm within him, and off he would go. Arnie received virtually no training. He had to train himself. He was always looking for information and tips that would help him to be more successful.

Arnie and I had a trusting relationship. He knew I would give him my honest opinion, but in a positive and supportive way. He didn't have to be afraid that I resented the fact that my life wasn't easier than it was. I wanted him to succeed for the sake of our

41

mutual success, not for my own ego. Arnie was given the freedom to open up, to be vulnerable, without fearing that I would be unkind or would put him down.

Family Matters

Some women ask why I seem to have given up so much of what they would call independence and self-fulfillment by always being there for my family, and not putting my own needs first. I didn't see it as giving up something, even though I didn't pursue a career outside the home. I had first received the gifts of unconditional love and time from my parents, even though we didn't have much in terms of money. I wanted to make that same investment in my own family. It is a tremendous accomplishment to be a positive influence in the lives of others.

My mother, Laura, and father, Fred, always put family first. That had a big influence on who I was and how I undertook my own role as a caregiver. Their example nurtured my desire to be a supportive wife and mother. I can't remember a time when they weren't thinking about how to care for our family and our home. Mom was always at home, baking and canning. I believe that's why I chose to be at home for our daughters and even carried on her home-baking tradition. It was important to be home when the girls were. Now Joan and Vicky are following the same path. They are college graduates who chose to stay home and nurture their families—they are even baking!

Staying closely knit and being available for each other was always a great reward. In northern Minnesota, relatives grew up close together, often on adjoining land, because of the patterns of settling and developing the land. One area might be predominantly Swedish, another Serbian, another Finnish, and so on, but even these were linked by work and social associations. Social life centered on extended-family activities. We knew nearly everything there was to know about one another, both family and neighbors.

Because of this upbringing, doing things together was as natural as breathing. Arnie and I didn't have our own private agendas or expect to go off and do our own thing separately. We didn't see this as a penalty, but as the natural scheme of relationships. We didn't have many entertainment choices, so the activities we enjoyed—from playing cards, to picnics, to camping outings, or parties—involved communication.

Arnie and I planned our lives during our time together, such as during mealtimes. We shared our experiences; we laughed and planned both our work and play. Our ability to think of one another and support one another came from this upbringing. Too many people put themselves first, asking, "What can I do that's pleasing to me?" That kind of thinking can stifle togetherness in a marriage. Spouses can be left feeling it's not worth sticking it out.

A lot of people claim their spouse is their best friend. I hope that's true—it was with Arnie and me. We did most things together, except hunting. When the majority of one's non-working life is consumed with things that keep people apart rather than bring them together, trouble often lies ahead.

We recently returned from Arnie's high school class reunion (Class of 1956). The majority of the married couples we knew from our years on the Iron Range were still married. Many had come from environments similar to ours, with a focus on family. The durability of these marriages seems contrary to the trends that we see today, but it reaffirms my instincts on the importance of families.

Despite what might have appeared to an outsider to be a bare bones, near-poverty existence, Arnie and I didn't feel sorry for ourselves. We kept looking ahead and moving forward. Some people in our position were either content to accept their present lifestyle, or they didn't believe that a dream of a better lifestyle was possible. There is a path one can follow. Arnie can think about and focus on a dream long enough to be certain that he wants it. When he can almost see it, smell it, and taste it, then it is no longer a dream, but a goal—something that he devotes himself and his energies to reaching.

Many people spend their time judging how insurmountable an obstacle may be. Arnie and I spent our time evaluating how to get around obstacles. We viewed them as challenges and opportunities. As easy as our life is today by comparison—when we look back at those times of struggling—that is when we were truly at our best.

PART TWO

"By acting with enthusiasm, we can actually become more enthusiastic and positive—traits that have the power to change lives."

CHAPTER SIX

To Be Enthusiastic, You've Gotta Act Enthusiastic

Many years ago, when I was trying to establish a niche in the business world by selling retirement plans to employers, one of my prospects paid me a huge compliment: "Arnie, I'm not sure I completely understand what you're trying to sell me," he said, "but you're so enthusiastic about it, it must be good, so I'll buy it."

I wasn't surprised that he didn't fully understand what I was selling. As a matter of fact, I'm not sure I did. Not that I was trying to scam him or sell him something I didn't believe in. I knew enough about retirement plans to be confident of their value, and I could present their most important points to prospects and clients. But I didn't understand retirement plans as well as I should have. The training I had received from the insurance company I worked for was very limited, and retirement plans are much more complicated than most insurance products. The only help I received was to be given a book on retirement plans and told to talk to the company's legal counsel if I had any questions. He, as it turned out, borrowed my book to learn about the plans himself. I found myself doing what I had done in so many other areas of my life. I had to teach myself. As complex as retirement plans can be, I sometimes wonder how I made any sales.

The sales prospect who responded to my enthusiasm by making a purchase is an example of one of the greatest benefits of that quality. He acknowledged that enthusiasm was the factor that ultimately influenced him. In this case, it closed the sale. There may sometimes be a fine line between influencing people and manipulating them, and we have to be on guard to behave ethically. The ability to influence others is important in our jobs, within our circle of friends, in our community involvements, and in how we raise our children—if we have them—sending them off safe and well prepared to thrive in a difficult world.

Enthusiasm does more than just influence others. It influences us! Enthusiasm can give us the drive and energy to do bigger and better things with our lives. Every day we are faced with choices, situations in which enthusiasm can play a role. Sometimes we don't even recognize that we are making choices.

Here's an example. It's late in the workday, and we have the choice of completing a task before going home or leaving it until tomorrow. The course of least resistance would lead us to go home and forget about the task until the next day. But if we're enthusiastic about our work, we might choose to stay and complete it. The benefit of the do-it-now attitude is obvious. Businesses that have such owners or employees become focused on doing what it takes to meet customer needs, rather than just meeting minimum performance standards. They become industry leaders rather than middle-of-the-pack competitors. What would you do? It is a choice. Enthusiasm is a factor in choices like this, and—over the long term—the consequences can be life changing.

Most of us want greater rewards from our jobs. But making that happen takes a commitment to being qualified and prepared when a door opens for us. It takes a willingness to make an effort today, with hope and confidence that there will be a reward tomorrow. Without enthusiasm, we'll have a hard time making, or keeping, such commitments.

Sometimes it doesn't even take a long or difficult commitment. When UPI had grown large enough to think about hiring its first personnel director (now Human Resources Department), I was asked by a real-estate broker if we had any management positions open. I told him we were planning to hire someone to handle personnel matters and hiring. Tom Rutske said he was interested, and I asked him to come and talk to me the next week, to see if he might be qualified.

Tom already had good people instincts, in part, from managing people in the real estate business. But he had not held a position where his primary responsibility was personnel, nor had he dealt with many of the complicated issues that come with that territory. Before our meeting, he went to the library and took home several books on personnel management. When we met, his enthusiasm and preparation impressed me greatly. He seemed to have a real command of the big issues in managing personnel in business. It wasn't apparent that this depth of familiarity had been so recently acquired! Tom, after being hired, proved himself to be a top-shelf personnel director. But without the element of enthusiasm, he wouldn't have impressed me as he did, nor would he have taken the steps to make the best impression possible and make himself the candidate who stood out.

What about interactions with your children? Consider a child excitedly trying to tell you about an accomplishment they're proud of or something that happened at school. Maybe it was scoring a goal in hockey practice, being given a part in a school play or talent show, or winning a spelling contest. Does the youngster get your enthusiastic attention, or does he or she have to compete for your interest with the evening paper, your cell phone, or other distractions? Your enthusiasm for them and their priorities plays a key role in their self-esteem and sense of personal worth, and, ultimately, in the quality of their relationship with you, and perhaps their future.

I recall a wrestling match in high school, one of the few that my parents were able to attend. My opponent's record and skills were intimidating. No one expected me to beat him. But knowing my parents were sitting in the bleachers gave me the enthusiasm I needed. My adrenaline was surging like a river in flood that night. When the match ended, my supposedly superior foe and I were deadlocked in a scoreless tie, but it was a clear victory. My parents' presence, their enthusiasm and—as a result—mine, were part of the chemistry that made possible one of my most memorable wrestling achievements.

In my efforts to sell retirement plans to employers, my weakness in technical knowledge could have stopped me cold. But I was determined to overcome it because I felt that retirement plan sales could be a promising career opportunity for me and also because I do not like being beaten. Rather than let a shortage of knowledge stop me, I studied hard to become more knowledgeable. As I worked to plug the knowledge gaps, I looked for another asset to balance my shortcomings. That asset was enthusiasm.

Pass It On

I shared enthusiasm with my employees on a regular basis. Like more and more business executives these days, I had an open-door policy—my door swung out. I would also walk around our company's buildings to meet and talk with employees. Among other topics, I would share the company's successes, such as landing new accounts. I did it with enthusiasm, and made employees feel that they were important enough to hear it personally, from the company's owner. Both the news and the way in which it was delivered generated employee enthusiasm.

Dean, a longtime employee, tells the story of when we first met after he started working at UPI. I saw him in the hall, stopped to shake his hand, and welcomed him to the company. Noticing that Dean wore a Mickey Mouse tie, I reached out and touched it, and asked, "Hey, do you want to sell your necktie?" Years later, he told me that through all the years he worked for me, he was never sure if I truly wanted to buy his tie. My approach sometimes left people questioning where I was coming from. It was just another one of my ways of having fun with my employees.

Enthusiasm is not limited to the corporate world. My father-in-law, Fred Bennett, whom I came to regard as a friend, was a great example of this. Fred also worked in the iron mines of northern Minnesota. Fred was a dragline and shovel operator—a job with a lot of responsibility—and he was a perfectionist. There are ways to do almost anything in the "best" fashion, even excavating or loading iron ore, and that was Fred's belief. Perfectionism is enthusiasm by another name. It's what makes a task that others might find repetitive and thankless, significant and rewarding. For

Fred, enthusiasm wasn't something he waited to have happen to him. He made a conscious choice to be enthusiastic, and made it a part of his life and work.

I can be a bit of a rabble-rouser, and I sometimes give myself the challenge of making a negative person behave positively, with my own enthusiasm. They may think I'm a pain at first, but I can usually win them over if I'm given enough time. The typical situation is when I'm dealing with a waiter or waitress, a teller or clerk, or some other person serving the public. When I encounter someone who's wearing a snarl on his or her face, or who doesn't bother to offer a greeting, I go to work. I usually start by asking, "How are you?" I turn on a warm smile, comment on the weather, and look for something to compliment about them or about their place of business. By the time I leave, I've usually received a genuine smile in return, and—with the beginnings of real enthusiasm—a farewell comment to, "Have a nice day." I admit that I do it to prove a point. But I have also paved the way for the next customer to be treated with warmth and enthusiasm. And maybe that person will pass it on.

Advice From a Duck

On the wall opposite the door of my office at Universal Pensions was a bronze plaque. On it was the likeness of a scowling cartoon duck, stamping its webbed feet, and shaking its fist-like wing tips in the air. Beads of sweat flew from its brow, as if it were warming up for a fight. From the duck's open bill you could almost hear it hurling a challenge. Below the image of the duck, in raised bronze letters, the words: "To Be Enthusiastic, You've Gotta Act Enthusiastic!"

This cartoon duck became a part of Universal Pensions' folklore. I discovered it in the mail many years ago. It had been mailed out by an insurance company that I represented as a motivational tool. The duck and its message was printed on a three-by-four-inch postcard. Despite the peculiar whimsy of the duck, its message has been one of the most important motivators in my life: "To Be Enthusiastic, You've Gotta Act Enthusiastic." In other words, by acting with enthusiasm, we can actually become more enthusiastic and positive—traits that have the power to change lives.

When we are enthusiastic and positive, we have the power to shape events and life around us. If we appear disinterested in life's events and opportunities, we will choke off enthusiasm. We will be left with little motivation. We will be passive and less able to influence our own future.

My belief in enthusiasm has been more important than the messages of the many motivational writers and speakers I've heard and read over the years. Enthusiasm was instrumental in shaping my career, first as a sales representative and later as founder and leader of Universal Pensions. Enthusiasm can be more important than our level of education, our intellectual gifts, or our manual skills. Enthusiasm is more important than our past successes or failures. Its presence—or absence—can make or break a company, a team, a marriage, and sometimes even the prospects for a community.

Think about the contrasts between the enthusiastic and unenthusiastic people you've met. Which ones stood out? Which ones would you rather be associated with? Which ones were able to influence you, and—as a result—benefit from their contact or relationship with you? When you go out for dinner, which waiters usually get the biggest tips? Is it the one who is enthusiastic and makes emotional contact with customers, or the one who acts as though serving customers is an inconvenience? At your medical clinic, do you prefer to see a physician who has shown interest in your health and your life, or one who rarely acknowledges you except when putting a tongue depressor down your throat?

Who attracts and holds the most loyal and active parishioners in a church or other place of worship? Is it a passionless, monotone member of the clergy who seems detached from parishioners? Or, is it the enthusiastic leader who is serious about delivering a meaningful message—enthused about playing a positive role in the lives of those who have come to him or her for spiritual uplifting?

Have you ever been in the position of interviewing candidates for a job? Recall what impressed you, or didn't impress you, about those people. I have little doubt that their enthusiasm—or lack of it—played a part in your decision. And, of course, we can't forget the classic example, the salesperson. Most of us don't want to be badgered when we're shopping. But we do want to be approached and recognized with warmth and enthusiasm, rather than ignored, or acknowledged coldly. Which salespeople, and ultimately which businesses, will be rewarded in the future? To which establishments will we refer our friends and associates? The answer lies in enthusiasm.

The enthusiasm of others affects how we act toward them—whether we reward them with our patronage, with a job or a promotion, with our attention, loyalty, friendship, or some other benefit. If this is how we respond to others, why would it not be equally true of how others respond to us? Just as we make judgments—responding in positive or negative ways to people we encounter—others do the same with us. Knowledge and talent are important. But enthusiasm is your secret weapon.

In the same way that my human resources director used his enthusiasm to sell me on hiring him, I've done the reverse, and used my enthusiasm to sell prospective employees on coming to work for UPI. Getting the best talent to come aboard, especially when a company is just starting out, can be difficult. Back when UPI had only a handful of employees and few clients, Tom Anderson (later to become UPI president), was working as a financial controller for a business in St. Cloud, Minnesota. I had heard very good things about Tom, so I contacted him to see if he would be willing to manage UPI's financial affairs.

But Tom already had a good position and wasn't interested. Changing jobs is always something to be considered with care, especially if you're leaving an established company to join a small company that has only been in business a couple of years. Tom's wife told him that he should "at least meet with Arnie," to see what UPI had to offer.

As you might expect of a good financial man, Tom asked to see our books. In my creative ingenuity, I found a way to stall him until after I had several opportunities to share my vision for UPI and how bright the future could be for him. Tom never saw the UPI financial statements before he said, "Yes." It's probably a very good thing, too!

I always tried to lead by example, and enthusiasm was no exception. Every few months we would hold an orientation session for newly hired UPI staff. We wanted them to know about the company's history and culture, how and where it began, how it had grown, and its guiding philosophies. We also conveyed our vision of UPI's future and the role that these new employees might someday play. My part of the presentation was the company's heritage. Besides the historical details, I always related the story of the duck. Employees not only heard the story behind this UPI symbol—delivered by me with great enthusiasm—but also received their own desktop cardboard duck.

Making Enthusiasm Happen

"But, enthusiasm is not my style," some readers might protest. Are you certain? Maybe you just don't think so. Most of us tend to label ourselves. Sometimes labels are based on good or bad experiences. Sometimes we've been labeled by others and have gradually accepted those labels. "Slow learner," "troublemaker," "dreamer," "victim," "shy person," "unenthusiastic," the list of labels could go on and on. After awhile, we begin to believe the label and act as if it's our destiny to be that kind of person. That is the thinking pattern we need to break out of.

I believe that by consistently acting in a certain way, we can eventually become more like the kind of person we want to be. We all know examples of behavior changes that have reshaped lives. Alcoholic or drug-dependent people who make a commitment to become drug or alcohol-free, who day-by-day embrace a new lifestyle, may not be totally free of their weakness. But they are nevertheless different people if they successfully change the destructive behavior. Smokers who kick the habit do not become nonsmokers on the first day they say "no" to nicotine. They become nonsmokers—free of the physical or psychological need to smoke—after a period of time spent living this new behavior.

Some people may resist this thinking. They may view attitudes and personality characteristics as unchangeable. But I have no doubt that our present attitudes and behaviors don't have to be our permanent destiny. The highly regarded book, *Psycho-Cybernetics,* written by plastic surgeon and psychotherapist Maxwell Maltz is based on this concept of change through conscious decisions and actions. The successes of many of his patients convinced him that change is possible by practicing the things we want to become. Enthusiasm is one of the ways we can put that strategy to work.

I've been successful in maintaining my motivation and my drive to succeed because I have cultivated an ability to generate my own enthusiasm, rather than waiting for enthusiasm and motivation to happen to me. You can do the same. Don't expect this to happen overnight—it didn't for me. Enthusiasm was natural in some parts of my life: as a skier, wrestler, and baseball player during my school days, as an angler and hunter, and even in some of my roles in the Army. But it was neither instinctive nor natural in other parts of my life.

When I left my job in the iron mines to earn a living in sales, almost everything about that life was different. I was enthusiastic about being independent, but I was unsure of the selling part, even though I believed it could be a way to reach my goal of independence. Selling was outside my comfort zone. Unlike driving a ninety-ton ore truck in the iron mines, I didn't feel as much in control when I was trying to make sales. I felt threatened.

How can it be done? Whether or not you've ever acted on a stage, you know at least a little bit about acting, because you've probably done it when required by everyday circumstances. Perhaps it was when you unwrapped a really ugly tie you received as a Christmas or birthday gift, and you smiled, despite the letdown. Or you acted nonchalant as you watched a nurse prepare a syringe for a vaccination, with a sensitive part of your anatomy the intended target. You've probably listened to a badly delivered joke and laughed anyway, as an act of courtesy.

Being enthusiastic when it doesn't seem easy or natural may require this kind of acting at first. But it works. It's also worth it, because there are some roles in life where it can make a big difference. For me, being in sales was one of those roles. I hoped enthusiasm would help me to overcome the anxiety I felt, trying to do something that was beyond almost all of my past experience.

When I practiced my sales presentations with Jo Ann, I worked on more than presenting facts and figures, speaking clearly, and asking for a commitment. I worked on adding enthusiasm. At first it felt forced. But, as I became more comfortable with the technical material and less anxious about my delivery, I found that—with all that practice—I had become enthusiastic. I felt less intimidated. I made the sales!

These days, when I'm delivering a speech to a group on the topic of business principles or motivation, I ask people in my audience to work on their enthusiasm. (They all leave with one of my 3" by 4" desktop ducks, too.) I ask them to try it at home or at work—not back-slapping or aggressive handshakes, nor a Pollyanna, "everything-is-perfect," attitude, either. I ask people for something more subtle and genuine, but performed consciously, and with purpose.

Try this: when your spouse asks you for help with a task at home, for your opinion, or for your company, put down your newspaper or magazine, click off the TV, and show him or her that you are paying attention and are interested in interacting. When your children are telling you about a school project, a test they aced, or merely a game of kickball on the playground, pay attention, listen, and respond with real interest. If a co-worker asks for your input or seeks your help on a project—or if there is an opportunity to take on responsibility or play a key role—do it with eagerness, as genuinely as you can.

Take enthusiasm initiatives yourself. Demonstrate your enthusiasm to a co-worker by asking if you can help with a task. If you play a supervisory role, look for opportunities to enthusiastically recognize good work or pay a compliment. Ask your children, before they tell you, "What was the best thing that happened at school today?" Approach your spouse to see if there is something that needs your assistance. Suggest something special for the two of you to do together. To some people, "trying" seems false. But I've found that by actively taking steps to be more enthusiastic—at work, at home, or in the community—enthusiasm becomes the genuine result.

The ability to generate enthusiasm—instead of waiting for it to happen—is one of the keys to shaping one's own life. This is true whether we are raising children or raising skyscrapers, whether we're trying to improve or redefine our job, or kindle a greater spark in our marriage. It's true at all levels of a business organization, from company owners to managers and down through rank-and-file employees.

There are opportunities all around us to show enthusiasm for others and enthusiasm for life in general. Enthusiasm is like love. The more we give it freely, the more we have, and the more it will be given back to us. And to be enthusiastic, you've gotta act enthusiastic!

CHAPTER SEVEN

Image Isn't Everything, but It's a Good Start!

One of my firmly held beliefs about life in general, and business in particular, is the importance of impressions. It would be nice if people placed less importance on image or appearances, and always reserved judgment about people or issues until they had all the facts. But unfortunately, that's not the way life works. We live in an age when we are bombarded with so much information, and have to deal with so many demands on our time that most of us have created screening tactics to keep the world at a reasonable distance. We do it so we can work and make decisions with fewer interruptions and demands on our time.

Do you ever sort through your mail and make judgments about what's inside, based on the appearance of the envelope? Do you sometimes decide against opening a piece of mail because, from the look of it, you've judged that it won't be worth your scarce and precious time? At work, perhaps a secretary or assistant examines your mail and screens your phone calls and unsolicited visitors, deciding who and what gets through, and what does not. When you get a telemarketing call from a credit card company during dinner, how do you react? You may have Caller ID to let you know whether the call is from someone you know, so you can decide whether to take the call. You may choose to let the "unknowns" leave a message, a message that you might—or might not—return. Whether it's mail, personal interruptions, or phone calls, most of us have established a process to identify what we will give our time to and what we won't. Most likely the decision is based on first impressions. It may be the appearance of an envelope, the name of a company, the sound of a voice, a person's choice of words, or their personal appearance. At some time or other, some or all of these are likely to be used to make time-saving decisions.

We're Judged, Too!

Guess what? The same rules we apply to others, also apply to us. You may be trying to get through to someone in order to show a product, get a job interview, solicit a donation, or accomplish a personal or professional goal. But unless you or your message is judged to be worth an investment in time or attention, you may be ignored. Your proposal, your resume, or your chances could be headed nowhere.

Stand Out from the Crowd

Standing out from the crowd is a big part of the solution. This doesn't mean you must completely transform your looks, dress, or personality, be a fraud, or pretend to be someone other than who you really are. It means making the most of what is unique, appealing, and special about you—perhaps meeting the expectations of others. It means paying attention to the first impressions you make, and to what it takes to make a good one.

As an insurance representative, I traveled thousands of miles across the farmland of west central and southern Minnesota. I would sometimes pull into a farmyard as early as 4:30 or 5:00 in the morning to set up a future appointment with the farmer, or to discuss a retirement plan or some insurance need. I did this because I knew the farmer would be milking cows or doing chores before it was light enough to be out in the fields. I met the farmer on his turf, according to his schedule, without making an immediate demand for his time.

My willingness to make this kind of effort impressed these prospects. Many of them seemed stunned that I would get out of bed early enough to be there to meet them, rather than expecting—as others did—the farmer to adjust his schedule. This strategy proved to be a door opener, a disarming tactic that made me stand out from the others who wanted a slice of the farmer's time and bank account. My strategy didn't always result in a sale, but I nearly always got an appointment and a chance to make my case. And, if nothing else, I always earned the farmer's respect.

Was I selling out? Was I sacrificing my integrity? No. I was using my intelligence and my willingness to make personal sacrifices in order to out-perform my competition. Competitiveness is a positive thing, unless you end up sacrificing your ethics or self-respect. I was sacrificing neither.

Image Matters

Personal appearance is where I may part company with some readers. Back in the 1960s and '70s, young people who wanted to be considered liberated from their parents' culture often attacked the rules and conventions accepted by previous generations. One of these conventions was appearance. "Dress for success" is not a theme that would have earned popularity points with most young people of that time. Wearing a suit and tie, cutting one's hair or beard, or grooming oneself to meet the expectations of the "establishment," were seen as selling out, sacrificing one's individuality, and integrity. The general attitude was, "If they don't like me as I am, too bad."

Many of the so-called independent young men and women of that time may have been exchanging the standards of their parents' generation for the standards and uniform of their own. The army surplus field jacket, hiking or combat boots, long hair, beards, and tie-dyed clothing, might have seemed like signs of independence from their parents' generation. But for many, these served as a membership card in their own generation's subculture. Ironically, some young people adopted this look in order to be accepted by their peers, while at the same time mocking those who conformed to the expectations of the business world, the world of their parents—a double standard, in my opinion.

Each person's individuality is important. But many confuse our individuality or uniqueness with our outward appearance. Just as looking polished and professional doesn't guarantee that we are professional, conforming to some of the expectations and norms of society—like appearance—doesn't mean a person has no ability to think independently, or has sold out and accepted a completely new set of values. Making an extra effort to create a good impression is not always selling out. It may just be smart.

The people and businesses to whom I later sold insurance, mutual funds, and retirement products had expectations about the type of person they would be dealing with. The financial-services industry at that time was a world of starched white shirts, ties, and vested suits. If I had called on prospective clients without a necktie, I wouldn't have gotten in the door. Styles and practices do change over time, however. The business world is a more casual place today than it was ten years ago. But when we decide how much we will, or won't, conform, we have to ask ourselves about our real mission. Is our mission to be successful at a professional task—to achieve a goal in life? Or is our mission to revolutionize the world?

Cadillac or Tractor?

When I would call on farmers out in sprawling western Minnesota, I was certain to catch their eye with the dark-green Cadillac I drove. Some farmers reacted with suspicion, a few with contempt. Few farmers drove Cadillacs in those days, at least in that part of the state. Some asked me how I could afford to drive such an expensive car, and perhaps wondered whether I might be getting wealthy at their expense.

But I was ready for their challenge. In fact, I sometimes counted on my Cadillac to provoke it. My answer was to make them an offer: I would swap my Cadillac for their best tractor (a tractor which often had a full cab, heat, air conditioning, and a high-fidelity sound system). The farmer reacted as though I'd lost my mind. How, he would ask, could he do his field work with a Cadillac?

"Exactly my point," I replied. "You need equipment that fits the job you have, and so do I. If you had to travel every day, covering hundreds of miles of dusty, poorly paved roads to meet and serve people like yourself, I bet you'd have a car like mine, too!" This comeback would usually break the ice and the corners of the farmer's mouth would turn up in a grin—or even a laugh—and the farmer would agree that I might have a point.

I found a creative way to set myself apart from my competition—a way to get my prospects' attention and get them to react emotionally. This is always a good start to a sales presentation. My boldness usually put us on an equal footing, creating warmth and acceptance between us, despite the great differences in the tools of our trades and the image we projected in our respective businesses.

Associating with Success

My clients and prospects understood the value of associating with success. I'm sure most would have admitted that they would rather deal with a professional whose products or services were good enough to make that person successful, rather than buying from a person who was not successful. A salesperson who is struggling in his occupation might be less knowledgeable, less committed, or offering products or services that are second rate. "Would you rather buy from someone who drives a well-maintained Cadillac," I asked, "or a beat-up, oil-burning old Chevy?" Case closed.

More than we realize or admit, we want to be associated with success. This isn't always a matter of snob appeal. As I told the farmers, a person, a company, or a product sometimes succeeds for a basic reason: it's better. While the appearance of success is not always a reflection of quality, the appearance of success is sometimes the only evidence we have to help us make choices. So we go with the odds and lean toward the signs of success.

We're more likely to stop for a meal at a roadside diner if there are lots of vehicles in the parking lot (especially trucks, so the theory goes). Or, if we're dealing with a medical issue, a physician with whom it is hard to get an appointment is probably more in demand due to greater skill or experience—compared to a colleague who has openings in his or her schedule the day after tomorrow. If you're buying wine for a party, it's widely accepted that a bottle of French wine with a five-dollar price tag will not be as good as a twenty-dollar bottle with a well-known label. This may not always be true, but in the marketplace, we often find that a higher price is often an indication of higher quality. Appearances, accessibility, perceived value—are all part of the look of success.

The same holds true with people. Looking and acting successful works in your favor. I felt so strongly about this that I once sent my daughters to a seminar for business professionals, on how to dress for success. I believe in highly polished shoes and may have even given Jo Ann some advice on starching shirts to U.S. Army standards. I believe in a firm handshake and making eye contact. All of these are elements of confidence and making a good impression.

But image and preparedness go hand-in-hand. Your important first impression is nullified if you are unprepared. I recall many instances when I've watched individuals drive into the UPI parking lot, get out of their car and put on their suit coat, or comb their hair, or take long minutes to freshen their makeup or review their notes before coming in to the receptionist. While I appreciate such persons' caring about the first impression they make, I would be more impressed if I hadn't seen them do it at the last minute, and right under my nose!

You Are in Sales!

Does making a good impression mean anything if you're not in sales, where making a good impression really counts? Whether you know it or not, everyone is in sales. You might be a freelance consultant, an hourly construction worker, a college student seeking a prized scholarship, a school teacher trying to motivate a class, or a neighborhood kid asking homeowners for their summer lawn-mowing business. Whatever you do, don't conclude that you're not in sales. In many of life's circumstances, whether professional, personal, or academic, each of us must sell ourselves in some way or another, in part, and our services, by making a good impression.

You may want a seat on the board of directors, a promotion to a preferred shift, or a great summer internship in college. Someone, or some organization, somewhere, sooner or later, will have something you want. You can't presume that all your qualifications and selling points are common knowledge.

There is not always a clear-cut choice—very little is black and white or absolute. When our future or our best interests are at stake, we must do what we can to influence how those interpretations and judgments about us, or our abilities, are made. How we present ourselves, the confidence we can create in the person or persons we need to influence, will often determine whether we, or someone else, will get the prize. Image isn't everything, but it's a good start!

CHAPTER EIGHT

Crisis or Opportunity?

As much as we like clear, positive answers to questions, what we call "facts," can often be interpreted differently by different people. You've heard the example of ten different people witnessing a car accident and each having a slightly different description of what happened. What's a fact? What's an interpretation? What do some people see that others don't?

Then there's the question: "Is the glass half empty or is it half full?" A psychologist is likely to label a person who says "half full," as an optimist—a person who expects good things. The person who says "half empty," is labeled a pessimist, one who seems to always be on the lookout for negative or unpleasant things in life.

The key to both examples is how people interpret what they see in front of them. In order to make our way through life, each of us gathers, sorts, and interprets information about the events around us in order to come to conclusions about life and to respond as needed. The information we gather, and how we interpret it, are based on our own experience, personality, and attitudes.

No matter how smoothly our lives seem to be going, there will be a time when something unexpected and unpleasant happens. How we respond may very well determine whether that event will have a negative or a positive effect on our lives. Is it a crisis? Or could it be an opportunity in disguise?

Most people live in fear of losing their jobs. Others can't

force themselves to take the sometimes-risky step of leaving their current job for something better. Too often we cling to the safe position, even though it may be unrewarding or unsatisfying, because it's familiar and gives us a safety net in a world where having a job means financial survival. If we could look at such situations with greater clarity, we might decide we'd be better off doing something else; we may be wasting skills and potential we could be using for even greater things. My own experience, having left a position in the iron mines of northern Minnesota when I realized that I had potential that would never be reached if I stayed there, is a good example.

I've also been on the other side of the fence and have had to make a decision affecting the future of an employee. At one point in the early years of Universal Pensions, we were forced to lay off a computer programmer because we were overstaffed in that department and couldn't afford to keep him on. All other work factors being equal, he was the programmer who had to be let go because he was the last hired and that was the fair decision to make.

After learning of his release, the programmer called me at home and pleaded to be kept on as an employee, even if it meant sweeping floors at the printing plant our company also owned. His emotion was so deep, I could feel the panic in his voice. He was a very bright person, and that was part of the reason I had to refuse. "Tomorrow will be a better day," I told him. "Trust me, you'll do well. Just don't sell yourself short."

I wanted him to understand that he should not be content merely to have a job, when he could have a rewarding career that made use of his potential. He later became the manager of programming for a regional telephone company. Although it was unpleasant for him to leave Universal Pensions, it proved to be a positive step. If he had stayed on with us in a role that was beneath his potential, he wouldn't have grown as a professional and as a person, and his self-esteem and accomplishments would not be what they are today. An event that must have seemed a major crisis eventually proved to be an opportunity for him.

Look For the Up-Side

In the earliest days of Universal Pensions, soon after I began providing retirement services to several small banks in central Minnesota, I came up with the idea of offering brochures to explain the basics of IRAs to their customers. At the time, I had no line of credit at a bank to help me over the cash-flow bumps. Instead, I had to rely strictly on what was in the company checkbook. More often than not, it was a case of what was not in the checkbook.

My first buyer was sold on the idea before seeing a finished brochure. As a sample, I had a folded sheet of typing paper, with a handwritten title on the cover and lines drawn on the inside to represent the brochure's contents (yet unwritten). Cash flow was such an issue that I needed to convince my customer—Farmers and Merchants State Bank of New York Mills, Minnesota—to place an order and also to pay me in advance.

I hoped the brochures would be a profitable new product for Universal Pensions. It was pretty disturbing when the printer called and left a message that the brochures were finished, but there was a problem. All sorts of unpleasant possibilities were swirling around in my head. Had I made a mistake in the brochure's copy? Would I have to fork over money for a product I couldn't sell?

When I met the printer, he handed me a sample. Before I could look at it closely, he told me he was sorry, and he would begin reprinting the job immediately. The inside of the brochure had been printed upside-down! Fortunately, it was his fault and not mine, but my customer's brochures would be delivered later than I had promised.

I began to see an opportunity. The printer asked if I might have any use for the misprinted brochures in addition to the corrected ones. I said I had no idea whether I'd be able to sell them, but I offered to take them off his hands, rather than see them thrown away. I purchased the upside-down brochures for pennies on the dollar. I left the printer's office, concealing the sparkle of opportunity in my eye, got into my car and headed down the road to try to make a sale!

When I showed the upside-down brochures to a client or prospect, I usually got a quick, and negative, response. My strategy was to suggest that this brochure would be especially effective. "It's a well-known fact," I said, "that most people take a quick look at information like this, and throw it in the trash if something doesn't catch their attention. But if people have to take a physical action, like turning the brochure right-side up," I continued, "they'll read it almost every time." On the strength of this logic, I managed to sell every one of those brochures.

Opportunity Breeds Opportunity

Sometimes one opportunity is connected to another. I realized that the bankers who purchased my brochures would also need a way to display them. An easel, perhaps? I couldn't afford to invest in having them manufactured, but I had another idea. I was looking for every revenue-generating product we could find, so it wasn't long before our garage at home began to look like a carpentry shop. Using a handsaw, I cut the easel pieces from oak boards. Jo Ann stained and varnished them. Some bankers received their easels with the varnish barely dry! I even capitalized on the traffic-flow patterns in many banks to boost sales. I let the bankers know they needed one for each door, so customers couldn't miss them no matter which door they used.

Crisis or Opportunity? You Decide

In *Psycho-Cybernetics*, Maxwell Maltz proposes that we can change our lives by changing our beliefs and our image of ourselves. Whether we end up with a crisis or an opportunity often depends on what we expect and how we react to a situation.

Maltz described a successful baseball relief pitcher. Of all the roles in sports, few are as pressure-packed. A relief pitcher is often called upon to perform when the game is on the line. There are pitchers who choke up in such situations and can't pitch as well as they can under more favorable circumstances. These are not the players a manager wants as relief pitchers in his bullpen.

Fortunately, there is also the kind of player who is the answer to a manager's dream, the one who earns a reputation as a "money player," or a "go-to guy." This is the pitcher who seems to be at his best when the situation is at its worst, when a crisis is looming. This kind of player wants to be called on when the outcome hangs in the balance.

Maltz asked one such athlete how he handled the pressure, how he managed to come through in the clutch so often. The pitcher told Maltz that when he entered the game, he tried to think about what he wanted to happen and about what he was going to do when his manager gave him the ball and told him that it was all up to him.

You can see an attitude at work here. Some players might approach the same situation with a crisis mentality, afraid of how they will perform, or afraid of what the opposing batters might do to them. But not this pitcher. He went into a game planning to be successful, analyzing and calculating what he needed to do to win. He wasn't wasting his precious mental energy wondering how he might fail. He was channeling his energy into determining how he would win. This is the kind of attitude we each should try to cultivate in ourselves.

"Positive" Shows

Test this yourself. If you have the opportunity to watch a truly good relief pitcher in a game, perhaps aided by the television camera's ability to zoom in close, look at the facial expression, the eyes, and the pitcher's overall manner. The best relievers are cool, intense, challenging the batter with an icy calm. If you see beads of perspiration, you know the pitcher is sweating confidence! Don't think for a minute that this outward confidence doesn't contribute to their success. It does! The batter at the plate sees the certainty, the will to win. Unless he's equally confident, he's at a disadvantage before he even lifts the bat off his shoulder. Top relief pitchers know how to win, and their certainty that they will win is visible, and contributes to that result.

Conquer the Crisis Impulse

The paralysis of fear—choking up—happens to many people. With the first signs of anxiety, some of us jump to the conclusion that we're afraid. We may believe that having a fear sensation is a sure sign that we are inadequate to handle the situation and are likely to fail. The trigger for such a feeling could be a speech or presentation we must make to a group of co-workers, a job interview, an athletic contest, an important exam, or any spotlight situation. If we seize on the idea of being inadequate to the task as soon as we experience any anxiety, we are likely to create a self-fulfilling prophecy. We may predetermine our own failure.

Don't Misjudge Yourself

Often the real problem is one of underestimating ourselves, failing to understand human nature. We misinterpret normal anxiety and see it as a sign of weakness. We dwell on it until it becomes full-blown fear. We allow it to absorb and consume us, until a calm, rational, and effective response to a situation is difficult—perhaps even impossible. We need to give ourselves a chance, give ourselves the opportunity to react positively. As President Franklin Delano Roosevelt said during the depths of the Great Depression, in perhaps his most famous quotation from a lifetime of memorable speeches, "All we really have to fear, is fear itself."

Johnny Carson, former host of *The Tonight Show*, predecessor of the likes of David Letterman and Jay Leno, and arguably the best-known name and face in American television for many years, has been described as being shy by nature. Carson admitted that, before the start of his show each night, he had butterflies in his stomach and many of the symptoms of anxiety felt by others who are about to move outside their comfort zones.

It helps to know that even famous professional performers share the feelings of uncertainty that we have. One big difference is that such people have come to regard anxiety as a cue—a call to action—rather than a calamity. Anxiety is a bodily response associated with a build-up of adrenaline, a sign that the body and mind are getting ready for an important event. We shouldn't interpret this as a signal that we're inadequate and about to fail.

Maxwell Maltz also wrote of world heavyweight boxing champion Jack Dempsey. Before a fight, Dempsey was so nervous, he couldn't control his hands enough to shave himself. He couldn't stand or sit still. But Dempsey didn't interpret this as fear or a sign of his inadequacy. He recognized it as a natural, nerve-driven lead-up to his particular form of battle. He didn't try to avoid the feeling or the opponent, and probably benefited from the additional adrenaline boost.

Most of the battles in our personal and professional lives are far different from these pressure-packed experiences. But they may generate a similar kind of emotional buildup. Rather than putting ourselves down for not being icy calm in such situations, we should remember Jack Dempsey and Johnny Carson. Rather than signalling failure, our butterflies and our rising level of adrenaline can help us meet a challenge ahead.

Look for the Silver Lining

In 1986, when Universal Pensions was barely ten years old, a new federal tax law looked as though it might rip the heart right out of the IRA business—business which was critically important to my company. The tax law changes made it much more difficult for the average American to receive a tax deduction for saving money in an IRA, and it was anticipated—correctly—that fewer Americans would put their savings into an IRA. This was a major blow to companies like ours that served the retirement industry. The question seemed not only how, but whether, we would be able to survive this blow dealt by Washington lawmakers.

I could have panicked, as some in our industry did. I didn't, because I had the advantage of having survived many ups and downs in my professional life. Years earlier, I left the security of the iron mines to take a chance as a construction contractor. When that first venture failed, I had to return to the mines. But I bounced back. I learned that you can always pick yourself up, dust yourself off, and try again. Later, I took another chance, leaving the mines for the insurance business. This time I was successful, and eventually carved out a different niche—serving the retirement plan market.

I had already experienced risk, uncertainty, and setbacks. Now, a decade later, with my company having grown and become relatively successful, the stakes were much higher. If workers stopped saving through IRAs, the companies that purchased our consulting, training, documents, software, and publications might not need our services. How we reacted to this challenge could decide the survival of our growing company, and with it, the financial well being of many employees and their families.

Truly, experience is the best teacher. Having previously proven to myself that I could rebound from setbacks, I was able to stand back from the anxiety of the moment, keep calm instead of hitting the panic button, and inspire confidence in those around me. I was reminded of the question that my first insurance mentor had asked when I was deciding whether to leave the mines to pursue the insurance business: "What is the worst thing that can happen to you if you fail?"

Could we fail now? If our worst fears came true, Universal Pensions might lose sales, shrink in size and stature; yes, perhaps even fail. Could we survive that? Could we start over if we had to? I knew that somehow we could. After all, we were already survivors. Once I recognized that, I was able to calm the fears in myself and in my company's managers and help us all to concentrate on how to make the most of the challenging opportunity that might lie ahead.

Our answer to this challenge was to shift gears and focus more on that part of the retirement market that had not been as radically affected by the legislation—business retirement plans—instead of focusing so heavily on IRAs for individual savers. We also quickly realized that even if IRAs should slump in popularity with the new restrictions, those banks, insurance companies, and the brokerages we served would need our help in understanding and adapting to the new rules in a changing market. We knew the rules and the market as well as anyone, and were positioned—at least in this time of transition—to perhaps be even more important to them than before. We used this strategy to guide our brainstorming and sales strategy. We did not give in to fear and panic. We realized that if we searched hard enough and optimistically enough, we might discover a silver lining behind the tax law cloud—an opportunity under a layer of apparent crisis. Instead of being a year of disaster, 1987 proved to be one of our most successful years ever.

Over, Under, Around, or Through

Like a successful relief pitcher, each of us will be more likely to succeed if we believe that we can only be beaten if we let ourselves be stopped. We are most likely to fail if we come to believe we won't succeed, and give up without looking for the options and alternatives that may be waiting to be discovered.

To make sure success is the result, I don't let myself be brought to a standstill. I keep moving forward and refuse to let a problem or obstacle prevent me from getting where we want to be. I once gave an interview on a local radio station after being named Minnesota Small-Business Person of the Year for 1989 by the U.S. Small Business Administration. When the radio interviewer asked me for some of the reasons for my business success, I replied, "When I encounter a problem, I go around it, over it, under, or through it."

Back at the office, Gene Patch*, a vice president of our company, had listened to the interview. He went immediately to our marketing department, and had them make up a sign with that statement on it. He was waiting for me when I returned from the interview, presented it with great fanfare, and said: "Arnie, this is you." He was right—that simple philosophy has been responsible for progress when progress should not have been expected, and for success when others predicted failure. In the end, when there is something we want badly enough, there is almost always a way. All we must do is find it.

* By way of reference, Gene Patch was appointed senior vice-president over our Universal Printing division. When we acquired Universal Printing, it had one full-time and two part-time employees, with $50,000 in annual revenue. When we sold it in 1998, it employed one hundred and was producing $10 million in revenue.

Cultivate Your Self-Assurance

Over the course of many years, I've developed the habit of trying to approach a problem without having a shred of doubt that I will overcome it. Not that everything I have attempted has succeeded. There have been setbacks. But I believe that nearly every obstacle is accompanied by some benefit. Sometimes the benefit is hard to see. It may be only the lesson of discovering you did the best you could, found out what didn't work, and learned what to eliminate and what not to try again. But that's important, too. For success to become more than just a matter of luck, we must each believe that we can—and will—be successful. We needn't leave success to the whims of good fortune or good timing. We must believe that persistence and faith will enable us to overcome obstacles, and that what we first see as a crisis may be an opportunity in disguise.

Transform Your Fear

Use your fears positively. Don't deny their existence, but recognize them as a cue, a call to action that can motivate you in a positive direction. Don't make the mistake of interpreting the sensation of fear as proof of your inadequacy—your inability to stand up to difficult circumstances. Take on your challenges aggressively, whether at work, at home, or in other areas of your life. Be determined to come out on top, and turn what appears to be a crisis into a creative opportunity. Believe that you can, and you will!

PART 2

CHAPTER NINE

Nurture the Dreamer

Among the handful of really important discoveries I've made in my life, one that I believe has great potential to change human lives, is the capacity to dream. Without the ability to dream, my life and that of my family would have been very different—and far less rewarding.

I might still be a worker in the iron mines, approaching retirement as a "lifer," rather than having spent a quarter century guiding a company that has become one of the nation's leaders in the field of retirement-plan consulting services. (Or, considering what has happened to the steel industry in recent years, I might be out of work!) Not that being a miner is anything to apologize for.

Mining is an honest, hardworking way to make a living, and a profession I once shared with my father, grandfather, father-in-law, several uncles, and many friends and acquaintances. I'm proud of that heritage. But the end result of my own dream—owning my own business—has been one of my life's greatest rewards, one that I would not have wanted to miss for anything. But I would have missed it, if not for my capacity to dream.

Many years after my high school graduation, I had a few former high school classmates say: "Arnie, you were always a dreamer." It's an expression that can have opposite meanings. Calling someone a dreamer can mean that the person has vision, imagination, and the gift of being able to see beyond the commonplace to find the new and the undiscovered. Or, sometimes, when we call someone "a dreamer," we mean he can't keep his mind on his work—an impractical person who isn't grounded in the "real world." Unfortunately, our society has an uneasy relationship with dreamers.

I suspect that most classmates who thought of me as a dreamer in high school were making the less complimentary judgment. I was not exactly a model student. I graduated in the bottom half of my class, perhaps because I didn't focus very much attention on studying. I focused instead on things that interested me more, like sports, the outdoors, and—like many teenage boys—girls.

I don't, by the way, recommend approaching school with that attitude today. With today's ever-changing technology and the rapidly changing world economy, education has never been more important. Traditional professional fields also require a long period of study, professions like medicine, engineering, or law.

Perhaps, and I say this only partly in jest, schools should offer a class entitled, "Dreaming 101." In such a class, students would be encouraged to set aside practical thinking and would not be criticized for being dreamers. They would be asked to put aside the attitude that their ideas or dreams must be goal-oriented, prof-it-oriented, or reasonable. Limits of that kind, and the value judgments they carry, can stifle creative thinking and can teach us to look for ideas and inspirations only within familiar boundaries. Real discoveries often lie outside the boundaries. When we can dream or can look at situations with fresh, unregimented minds, we're open to discoveries that are sometimes made as much by accident as they are on purpose.

The human mind is capable of so much, if we are encouraged to dream. I think America has a confused relationship with its dreamers. We claim to value the dreamer. We sing the praises of the inventor, the entrepreneur, the industrialist, the explorer, and others who have followed a dream to success. But it's often selective admiration. We seem to appreciate dreamers after they have become successful, powerful, or famous. That kind of appreciation is nothing more than jumping on the bandwagon. The real test of whether our society values dreamers lies in how much we encourage the process of dreaming—how favorably we treat those whose dreams are still being pursued, or have perhaps ended in failure.

Dreams or Credentials?

School is where I believe we should most actively encourage dreaming in our young people. We send them to school when their minds are most open to new ideas, and their imaginations are least restricted by adults' ideas of what is possible. I often wonder if schools have become a reflection of our performance-driven culture, with little time allotted to encourage dreaming. Today, as when I was in school, "dreamer" is likely to be a negative description of a child's behavior, a label meaning "unfocused," or "unable to concentrate."

Our society has become so concerned with having a formula of success for our young people that in some ways we've created narrow paths, hemmed in by fears of failure and pressures to conform. Kids' lives are dominated by schedules, leaving too little room for spontaneity or creative thinking.

As a society we seem to want our young people to take the right classes, get the right grades, perform at the highest levels on college entrance exams, participate in the right extracurricular activities, and build a superior resume before they've even graduated from high school.

Summer sports camps, language camps, and college-sponsored academic camps for high-scoring students, all contribute to a sense of regimentation and urgency at a very young age. This is very different from when I was young, when kids had time to wonder what they would do tomorrow, and most of their choices had more to do with fun than with furthering their future careers.

Many young people who are not straight-A students have something important to contribute. But how many programs are built around the needs and special talents of average students?

This is one reason why my company awarded scholarships for continuing academic or vocational education to high school students who did not get straight-A grades. In almost any school, there are "idea" people within the academic middle ground—creative young people who invent, create, and build. Their potential also deserves to be cultivated and reinforced.

I've heard that a number of years ago, a study comparing former students of the various colleges within the University of Minnesota revealed that (at least at that time) among the highest incomes were those earned by people who had once attended the University's General College. The General College had long been regarded by some as the place for goof-offs, underachievers, and—just maybe—folks of lesser intellectual potential. But perhaps these people had something else going for them, something that wasn't measured by test scores alone. Others may draw their own conclusions, but I have no doubt that hard work, personality, imagination, and the ability to dream played roles in these outcomes.

I don't advocate "dumbing down" education or lowering basic academic standards. Young people need to be prepared for a future that will be dominated by new technologies—perhaps entire new careers. But we need balance. We need to nurture the dreamer and his or her capacity to dream.

Nurture the Dreamer in You

It's never too late to revive, or inspire, the dreamer within you. Many people have successfully made radical career changes, or created their own careers, at age fifty and beyond. Many have also mastered new non-career skills or developed interests that enriched their lives at ages well beyond this. All that limits us is our own belief that it's too late.

How can you nurture the dreamer? How can you expand your personal universe of possibilities? Maybe it's not a major career move, but a sideline or moonlighting profession. Perhaps it's your own consulting business that takes advantage of a skill or special background. Disregarding profit and practicality, it might be a sport or a hobby that fascinates you, but from which you've shied away because you've been afraid to take the plunge. It might be a social cause, political activism, or a deeper exploration of philosophy or faith. Meaningful involvement in such interests is driven by motivation and commitment. Motivation and commitment, in turn, are preceded and inspired by our dreams.

Nurture the dreamer within you. Listen to the inner urgings

and instincts you may have been unconsciously trying to silence. Get back in touch with your dreams, old or new, and pursue them. Use the support of those who share your dreams—those who believe in you—to encourage you to take the first difficult steps and to help see you through. Remember, many small steps will get you to the same place that a few large steps will take you.

Each time we nurture the dreamer within us, that dreamer becomes stronger and more alive, able not only to dream bigger dreams, but to be more confident, more able to make them come true.

CHAPTER TEN

Ten-a-city

When our two daughters, Joan and Vicky, were growing up, they were exposed to the world of business almost every day. It was unavoidable, because Jo Ann and I have always collaborated closely in guiding our businesses. We openly and regularly discussed business issues—financing, marketing, new products, staffing decisions, and all the rest. I would come up with an idea, or what I thought was a genuine inspiration, and Jo Ann—a calm, insightful evaluator, and a person of great intuition—would offer her perspective, raise questions, play devil's advocate, and perhaps offer alternatives. Together we were a formidable team. And the place where this exchange of ideas usually happened was in our home.

In addition to what Jo Ann and I learned about school events or our daughters' relationships with friends, our daughters would hear about the "ins and outs" of business. This often happened during dinner, or when Jo Ann and I had our brainstorming sessions over morning coffee on weekends, or when we traveled together as a family. Rather than being shortchanged by being exposed to these business discussions, our children received a bonus and had more than just the normal interactions between parents and children. They received a practical business education, too.

Why was this valuable? In many ways, the habits of good business are habits that are good for living, too. Planning ahead, weighing options and outcomes, thrift, having and showing concern for other people and for things beyond ourselves—these are just some of the positive things that can be learned in managing a business. These are life values, which, in the case of our daughters, were learned in situations that were real, rather than presented as abstract rules or theories in a business course.

My Eleventh Commandment

When it comes to rules to live by, one of the commandments of my life and business is tenacity. It's a philosophy that was modeled for my children very early in their lives. Tenacity is the ability to remain committed to a goal, even when the challenges you face seem overwhelming.

One of my children, very young at the time, tried to pronounce the word, and it came out "*ten*-a-city" instead. This way of pronouncing it stuck, and, although this became our inside joke, there was never any doubt about what the word meant. We all understood it to mean that if people want something badly enough, if they think and behave as if they are unstoppable, this quality of tenacity will help them to eventually achieve their goal.

Don't Ever Give Up

Maybe you've seen the cartoon that once made the rounds of many workplace bulletin boards and washrooms. The cartoon shows a frog with its head down the throat of a heron-like bird with a long, sharp bill. The frog's rear legs are pointed up at the sky, and its webbed front feet are clamped firmly around the throat of the bird to keep from being swallowed. The caption reads, "Never, ever, ever give up." The message is clear: no matter how grim a situation appears, you still may have a chance—even if it's a small one—if you refuse to give up.

Winning with Tenacity

A very successful coach once gave his opinion that the only thing we learn by losing is how to lose. I disagree. If that were true, then athletes would not get better with experience, which many do. School children would not get better grades by improving their study habits, an ability that so many have demonstrated. Or people who fail to kick a self-destructive habit the first time they try would be doomed to a life of weakness and dependence. Yet most of us know of people who have tried, failed, tried again, and finally succeeded in ridding themselves of destructive habits or dependencies.

Unlike the cynical coach, I believe we can afford to fail, that we can afford to make errors in life. We needn't win at everything we do every time we try. What is important is what we do after we have lost. Quitting, rather than losing, is what makes a person a loser. Trying, and trying again if necessary, is what makes a person a winner.

Catching Your Dream

When I was a young man, one of my big dreams was to play first base on our baseball team. My dream was big, but my size was small, and I was beaten out for that position by a teammate. Not just any teammate, but—adding insult to injury—one of my cousins. But I didn't give up. I looked for other options that might also be rewarding. I tried out for, and won, a position as catcher on our team. Then I set out to become the best catcher I could be.

In a surprising way, I was probably more valuable to my team as catcher, because that position allowed me to become the player who could most effectively rattle and unnerve the opposition. This seemed to be the case, anyway, because every time I came to bat, the players on the opposing team would all come out on the dugout steps to heckle me. Their angry response was my payoff!

Was this the success I first wanted as a ballplayer? Not exactly. Success had been redefined a little from my first ambition. I was a catcher, not a first baseman. But the end result was a great success and came about because I was tenacious about making the team and playing an important role, whatever that role might be.

Dare to Fail

Following a short career as a lumberjack after being stationed in Iceland with the U.S. Army, I became a miner on the Mesabi Iron Range near where I grew up in northern Minnesota. But I ached to be independent and to do something else—something rewarding, with a more promising future. I finally took a chance, left the mines, and joined a friend as a partner in an excavating business. We didn't exactly take the Iron Range by storm, and after a short time it became clear we were not going to make it together. I was forced to bail out, to swallow my pride, and apply for another position in the mines.

It's after just such a failure that many of us lose our determination. I've known others who left positions of security to venture into business on their own. But once they have tasted defeat or disenchantment, many will never again try to make it independently. They will swallow their pride and their discontent, and resolve to live in a professional world that may be the lesser of two evils. The other evil, the one that scares them the most, is the risk of another failure.

I could have made that decision, too. After returning to the mines, where I eventually became a truck driver, I could have put aside my dreams of independence, counted the years ahead to retirement, and lived a relatively predictable, if not ideal, life. But that was not the path that I, rather I should say, we, chose to take. Jo Ann was as independent in spirit as I was. Despite having two children and facing all the usual responsibilities and challenges of family life, Jo Ann still encouraged me to look for new options. When a part-time opportunity to sell insurance came along, Jo Ann was my most enthusiastic supporter. She remained just as supportive when it came time to consider going full time in the insurance business, when I made a second risk-filled break from the mines.

I had been bloodied in my first attempt at independence, but we were unbowed—determined to find a way to reach our goal of self-determination and a better life. We lost that battle once, but did not feel we lost the war; we did not feel like losers, because we refused to accept that definition of ourselves. In order to achieve success, we were convinced that all we needed was time, a good opportunity, and tenacity.

Mutual Success

The sometimes-fickle fortunes of business had led me to leave the excavating partnership. But, as a positive note, my former excavating partner, Bill Schwartz, had the same quality of tenacity that I had. Just as I had been forced to return to the mines, Bill, too, found it necessary to find other work to support himself and his family. He farmed, worked in the mines in Babbitt, and worked in the woods as a logger, but he kept his dump truck and did excavating work on the side. He worked seven days a week for much of his life. While I finally succeeded in building a profitable pension company, Bill eventually established one of the most successful excavating and contracting firms in that region, and is now enjoying the fruits of his tenacity, just as I'm enjoying the fruits of mine.

Never Too Young

In the early days of Universal Pensions, when our staff and facilities were a fraction of what they were to become, I remember a young woman who applied for a job. She was about eighteen— just out of high school, I presumed. We had no openings at the time, but she was tenacious. At first she came back every couple of weeks or so. Still no positions were open. But rather than come back less frequently, she came back more often! According to the person who was then doing the hiring, she always had a reason, such as, "I remembered something that's not on my resume, and wanted you to know about it." Or, "I heard from a friend that you'll be hiring soon."

After a while, I found myself rooting for her, thinking, *Here she comes again. I hope we have something for her this time.* Our company's growth eventually resulted in our having an open position, and we hired her.

This girl reminded me of the job-seeking persistence I had after I graduated from high school, shortly before I left for basic training in the Army. In the miner's union of that day, it was possible to maintain priority for a job if you worked in the mines before going into the military. The requirement was thirty days of service on the job. I applied for a job at the Danube Mine near Bovey, but they weren't hiring. I came back a week later and spoke to the mine superintendent, and there were still no jobs. I came back one week later, still nothing. But instead of giving up, I began to come back each day!

After three or four days of coming to the mine each morning, I began coming to the mine every morning and every afternoon. On the second day of these twice-daily appearances before the superintendent, my unbelieving ears heard him say, "Come with me." I was given one of the lowest jobs on the totem pole—working in an iron-ore washing plant. But I had a job, and would be maintaining seniority while I was away in the military, which was my objective all along. Other people might have worried about being a nuisance and about hurting their chances for a job, but my instincts told me that I wouldn't get what I wanted by being invisible or shy. I needed to stand out from the crowd with persistence and tenacity.

Some believe that when we achieve success against great odds, we've risen above our limitations, that we're "playing over our heads." I believe the opposite. I believe most of us have greater capabilities than we imagine, capabilities that are just waiting to be discovered. Tenacity is the habit we develop to push ourselves to go beyond the obstacles, including the boundaries that we, or others, may have set for us. In Jo Ann's and my life, tenacity led us to discover that we are capable of, and worthy of, much greater things.

The Image of Success

In Brainerd, Minnesota, where UPI is based, lives a nationally known nature and wildlife photographer. Bill Marchel used to work in a small glass repair shop, but he didn't like the work much. He hoped for better things.

He dreamed of becoming a full-time nature and wildlife photographer and began to work toward his goal in his spare time. He examined nature magazines to learn what the photo editors were buying and budgeted to purchase the best equipment he could afford. He would trudge with heavy equipment through hip-deep marsh water to get better photographs of ducks and geese. While others were content to shoot pictures from the comfort of roadways or visitor observation platforms, he once built a tiny concealment blind and sat for days in its airless, mosquito-infested confines waiting for a grouse's eggs to hatch.

Today, Bill receives national awards for his wildlife photography. He was a finalist in *Life* magazine's Photographer-of-the-Year competition and is now so respected for his knowledge and skills that editors call him to consult on photo projects. Bill earns several times what he did as a glass cutter and has a bright future ahead of him.

Success wasn't made for Bill—success was made by Bill. He earned it—with tenacity!

Tenacity Will Work for You

Tenacity is not something that's important only for people going into business for themselves. It's vital to anyone who has a goal that seems difficult to reach. It helps with nurturing a better relationship with your spouse or your children, or preparing yourself to gain the credentials for a promotion where you work, or to land a different job. Tenacity can be applied to public speaking, or overcoming a fear that has haunted you all your life, or making a commitment to improve your health. Tenacity is not just for entrepreneurs. It's for everyone. And it works!

CHAPTER ELEVEN

Be Careful What You Really Want— That's Probably What You'll Get

Why would anyone not want his desires to come true? Perhaps the answer lies in understanding that each of our lives is a long parade of wants, whims, and desires. Some of the things we wish for may be good for us, some not. Sometimes we can't even be sure. Some attractions are weak and may soon vanish, perhaps never to return. Others become a repeating theme in our lives and can even change our life's direction.

Sometimes one desire conflicts with a second desire. For example, an attorney who wants to devote his or her life to representing the poor or underprivileged is probably not going to become wealthy. Yet that attorney might have a more rewarding life in other ways, with a different, but equal or greater, payoff. In a similar way, it wouldn't be realistic for someone to hope for a life as a highly paid stockbroker on Wall Street if that person hates crowds and big cities and doesn't want to put up with high levels of stress. Some wants are compatible, and some are not.

The more we dwell on a want or desire, allowing or actively causing it to become the focus of our life, the more likely it is that we will make changes in our lives to reach it. Changes may lead us toward one set of possibilities, while at the same time directing us away from others.

Whim or Want?

Some people make no distinction between wish, whim, want, or any other term used to describe something we are seeking. I do make such distinctions. I make them because I believe the intensity of our seeking sometimes does make a difference in whether we get it. In some cases, this actually works against our other goals—preventing us from reaching important objectives in our lives.

I define wishes and whims as things that come and go without much thought or focus, without great emotion or longing for them. When I was a young athlete in high school, one of my wishes was to be taller than my five-foot six-inch stature. But, having been shortchanged in the game of genetic roulette, I wasn't likely to have that wish fulfilled! At times, we all find ourselves wishing for things we can't change.

Wanting Can Make Things Happen

Wanting, by my definition, is more powerful—something to be taken seriously. It is a matter of greater focus—dwelling on and deliberately thinking about what we seek. Wants go deeper than whims or wishes. While we might not always be conscious of it, wanting involves our emotions as well as our thoughts. If a "want" becomes part of our thinking over a long period of time, it will likely lead us to take action, even unconsciously, to make it come true.

As a youngster I loved sports, and wanted to be athletically competitive. While I wished that I had been born with something a little closer to the classic athlete's body, I knew this was impossible. But the desire to be competitive was realistic. My wanting was powerful enough to shape my thinking. I actively thought about it, daydreamed about it, and imagined my success. It was something I truly and deeply wanted.

I couldn't play center on my high school's basketball team or linebacker on the football team. But wanting to compete led me to explore other possibilities and discover other opportunities for similar success. I channeled my competitive desire into wrestling, skiing, and baseball. These were pursuits I could excel in, even though I was small in stature.

I learned from this, and from similar experiences, that when our awareness and thought patterns are consistently directed toward something we deeply want, we begin to think and act with that priority in mind. We take steps that, by the miraculous power of will, can lead to that want coming true, in one form or another.

The Power of the Subconscious

We generally do not give enough credit to what our mind is capable of doing with a thought or a concept. Mental habits are as powerful as physical ones. Repetition of thoughts can influence our attitudes and behavior. The more our mind dwells on an objective, whether it's good or bad for us, the more likely it is to become a high priority in our life. Eventually, our subconscious becomes programmed to seek ways to make the want come true.

As I've already mentioned, Maltz's *Psycho-Cybernetics* was based on this belief. This human characteristic can be compared to the self-correcting guidance system of a torpedo or the programmed flight route of the auto-pilot mechanism of an airplane—a mechanism steering a course that will be followed by the plane without the pilot's attention or operating of the controls.

Because our wants and our unconscious goal-seeking behaviors work together to influence the direction of our lives, it's extremely important to deeply want only the things that are really important to us. One's life holds only a limited amount of time, energy, and resources that can be applied to the pursuit of wants and dreams. It's not possible to have everything in life that we would like to have. As unwilling as we may be to accept this, many of the choices we make bring unavoidable trade-offs.

There may be things we must give up to fulfill a different priority. Some wants are compatible with each other and can perhaps all come true. But others, which may be in conflict, can undermine our efforts and prevent our reaching some of our important goals. The trick is to know which things in life—which "wants"—to focus on.

Making Tough Choices

My own life might be a good example of having to make choices and accepting the unavoidable trade-offs. Growing up in northern Minnesota, it's not surprising that I was a hunter and fisherman. I especially liked duck hunting, deer hunting, and camping with my family. I was also an avid archer.

Yet, as much as these activities meant to me, spending time enjoying them was not how I used most of my so-called "free time" during the early years of our marriage—both while our two daughters were growing up, and when I was working hard to build Universal Pensions. Sacrifice was necessary in order to reach the goals on which Jo Ann and I had set our sights.

Instead of immediate rewards, like more hunting and fishing time, or more time for us to do things as a family, Jo Ann and I focused on what we wanted most—a more secure future. It was becoming clear that what was best for us was independence, a career or business that would reward me in proportion to how hard I was willing to work, rather than a seniority-based, low-incentive job that limited my opportunities. To reach this independence, I knew that sacrifices would have to be made.

Choices that seem unimportant may have bigger consequences, and affect the way we make similar decisions in the future. I recall a trip I once made to see a client in the rural town of Pierz, Minnesota, not far from Brainerd. With me was an attorney, my friend, Glen Gustafson, whom I needed to help my client. As we set off in my car on the forty-minute drive, Glen suggested that we turn on the radio and listen to the Minnesota Twins baseball game. He was quite surprised when I told him we were going to listen to a motivational tape!

Whatever it took to gain an edge, I pursued tenaciously. Even small choices like this set a pattern in how I pursued priorities.

Ripple Effects

Putting off immediate gratification for long-range goals affected other peoples' lives as well as my own. It wasn't simply a matter of turning down a weekend fishing or hunting trip—my family was affected by the sacrifices, too. When I was just beginning to sell insurance and securities, I felt it was important to make an impression of success on potential clients in order to gain their confidence and secure their business. At the time, we owned a nine year-old Ford—not the mark of a successful agent. I sold our family's boat so I could afford to trade in the aging Ford for a newer one. It was a sacrifice, but one that eventually paid off.

There were other personal sacrifices, too. Jo Ann believed I had the instincts and motivation necessary to be successful in an independent business venture, so she chose the primary, nurturing roles of homemaking and child-rearing. With her help and guidance, I was to be the entrepreneur.

I missed out on many daily family activities, little things that bind a family together and give life the richness of shared successes and disappointments. Joan and Vicky really had no choice in this sacrifice. It meant their father wasn't around a great deal to give them the time, patience, and understanding that comes with sharing everyday experiences, large and small. When I was at home during that period of actively building my business, I often had to rob the girls of some of their mother's time, too. I needed her to critique my ideas, offer ideas of her own, and listen to and help perfect my presentations.

Yet in important ways, our daughters were our first priority. For example, during her grade school years, our daughter Vicky earned the right to compete in New Orleans in the Little Miss Pageant. Rather than take a true family vacation that year, New Orleans became our vacation, because we couldn't afford to do both.

I believe Joan and Vicky also learned things from my experiences. I've shown them the results that can be achieved with tenacity, hard work, and goal setting. I've passed on my belief in the importance of strong family values, no matter how each partner's responsibilities might be divided, or what obstacles a family may face.

In adding up the contributions that Jo Ann and I made to our daughters' personalities, I hope our teamwork provided a good example. As I reflect on our daughters' approaches to life, I see two women who do not necessarily ask, "What would my mother and father do?" Instead they have become individuals with their own goals, applying the principles of independence, tenacity, and follow-through in which Jo Ann and I believe so strongly. That makes us proud and confirms that we have done many things right.

Loss or Investment?

At the time I was making these choices, I didn't view myself as a martyr, or someone who had been denied the good things in life. Jo Ann and I were focused on the future. Perhaps most important, our focus was on the things that would be possible if our dreams came true, rather than on the often tedious and energy-draining daily tasks we faced. I believe that envisioning a long-term result is the secret to overcoming present challenges to reach future rewards.

Each of us must constantly visualize the rewards we want in order to make them seem real and reachable. This is what provides the motivation to get out of bed each day with enthusiasm and commitment, whether making a sales presentation, being interviewed, or dedicating time to the needs of others. I don't believe success is always a matter of possessing natural skills or God-given intelligence. I'm convinced it's all about motivation and how we generate our own motivation. I compare it to a chain reaction, one that begins with wanting, imagining, and believing in the possibility of achieving an objective. The wanting and the believing drive our motivation, which in turn drives decisions and sacrifices that may be necessary to transform "want" into reality.

Jo Ann and I could see the potential for great rewards in the future—rewards that would follow the sacrifices we might have to make in the present. We saw a professional and personal destination that was more likely to be reached if we dedicated as many resources as we could—resources of time and our limited financial means—to pursuing that destination. Because we had clearly defined what we wanted and could imagine in detail what it would be like when this had been achieved, we could unwaveringly pursue these long-term life goals with the power of our own free will, and do it with enthusiasm.

Pulling in the Same Direction

I can't emphasize too strongly that what we have achieved would have been extremely unlikely for two partners who were not equally committed to the same goals. When mutual commitment is absent, being partners may be even more difficult than pursuing a goal alone. Like two horses pulling a wagon in different directions, little progress is likely to be made. One person's efforts can be undermined and undone if the partner has different goals. In such a situation, faith and enthusiasm can quickly become frustration and defeat.

Couples or partnerships that have a deep, cooperative commitment are extremely blessed. It may not be something that people can simply decide to do. Cooperative commitment takes genuine belief in common goals in order to make sacrifices and tough it out through difficult times. Partners with different values and goals, and who merely agree to "give it a shot," will probably not have the stamina to remain faithful to hard-to-reach goals when they face obstacles that seem too big to overcome.

You either have these shared values and ambitions by sheer good luck, or you are drawn to someone who shares your values and ambitions. If not, you may face an uphill battle when mutual commitment is needed.

Go for It!

When we're faced with a choice that has risk, we can be cautious and hold back, or we can take a great leap of faith and trust our resourcefulness to pull us through. There may be no foolproof way to determine the best course. But one thing is certain. If we always hold back, we will miss many opportunities. One of the things my wife and I had wanted since we first lived in the Brainerd area, was to own a home on Gull Lake. We had often taken Sunday drives as a family. Sometimes it was to look at the countryside. But it was just as likely to include looking at homes, setting those dreams in motion. It took a while before we took seriously the possibility of living on Gull Lake, but eventually we did.

Gull Lake is a large, scenic lake, excellent for fishing, sailing, power boating, and even great restaurants. One day we learned about a very nice home for sale and went to see it with a realtor. From the moment we walked into the entry, before we had a chance to see another room, we felt that this was home.

Later, away from the emotional influence of being inside the home, we admitted to ourselves that we probably couldn't afford it. We gave ourselves a few days to collect our thoughts and to think of as many pros and cons as we could. Still uncertain, Jo Ann and I went to dinner at a favorite restaurant on the lake to talk it over. As we sat there trying to make a calm and rational decision, an impulse came over me. I told her: "If we want it bad enough, Jo Ann, we'll find a way."

We knew we were going out on a limb and ignoring common sense, but we decided, over dinner, to take the risk and go for it. For the first year after we bought this home, a great share of my income went toward making our house payment. We struggled and had to cut some corners. But, in the end, we shakily managed to get by until my business revenues caught up with our dream. Is a leap of faith like this always a good move? Perhaps not. But if we always take the safe and certain path, there are a lot of experiences we'll never know. Jo Ann and I acted on a deep desire, went after something we wanted badly, and made it work.

A Path Not Taken

Others may want different things, and will choose different paths in order to pursue what they believe will make them happy.

My younger brother, Gary (who is now deceased), loved to fish. He took advantage of nearly every opportunity to go fishing. Gary was an excellent fisherman. But there were other things in his life he didn't have, things that I think he would have wanted, had he lived longer.

Gary was getting what he wanted in life. He really did want a life in which he could pursue his fishing passionately. By having this kind of preoccupation, he made decisions and ordered his life in such a way that he was able to do more of what was immediately rewarding to him. For some people, this is the measure of a successful life. I won't say that such an approach to life is wrong. For some people, Gary's path might bring the greater reward. But making choices mean trade-offs. Each of us must decide what makes life worth living for us. In making these choices, we must be willing to live with the results and not be tempted to look back, wishing we'd made different choices and done things differently.

My Reward

For the majority of my adult life, I focused most of my wants and my energy on achieving success in business. There were things that I missed along the way, like opportunities to enjoy some of my favorite pastimes, and many hours of time with my family. On the other hand, what did my family and I get in return? Our business gave my family security and many enriching opportunities. We've been able to travel widely, to experience other cultures and lifestyles, and to gain a greater appreciation of our own life and culture. We've shown our children that dreams can come true when you apply vision, commitment, and hard work to achieving those dreams. We've enjoyed many of the rewards that success, at least by the traditional definition, can bring.

Today, I'm able to do everything I denied myself in those years of struggle, and more besides. I've fished and hunted in many places in Canada and Alaska—places I might never have gone without the freedom given me by greater financial independence.

Homes in Colorado and Arizona, and trips to Europe, the Caribbean, and around the world have been possible, too.

Soul Searching

We need to know ourselves well enough to identify what we want most. We need to be realistic enough to judge what we may need to give up in order to get it. And we have to believe fully that it will be worth it. Unfortunately, many people do not plan ahead and make decisions with life's trade-offs in mind. They may not realize that by failing to make choices they are choosing a path in life by default. That path will lead them closer to one set of wants and farther away from others.

We need to recognize the role our most powerful wants play in shaping our lives. We need to take charge—defining what it is we truly want and acting upon it.

CHAPTER TWELVE

New Horizons

If there is one thing I've learned to expect in life, it is the certainty of change. Achievement and success are not the likely outcome of avoiding or resisting change, but of shaping change and adapting to it.

Universal Pensions, which Jo Ann helped me build into a powerhouse in the retirement-services industry, is one of the measures of my life's accomplishments. While it's unwise to measure one's self solely by professional achievements, it's foolish and unrealistic to discount the importance of our careers.

After a number of years as an insurance and securities broker, I realized the opportunities that had been provided by retirement plan legislation passed by Congress and enacted in 1974. I then founded Universal Pensions. From a one-person business with a handful of clients—clients who purchased IRA technical documents, brochures, and training services—UPI grew to be an employer of five hundred professionals, providing every imaginable service and product for IRAs and employer-sponsored pension and 401(k) plans.

On Monday, June 1, 2001, after a twenty-six year "marriage" to the company, I announced its sale. I hadn't run out of energy— at sixty-four years of age, I consider myself to have the vitality and ambition of some men half my age. The company was not in financial trouble. We had been profitable in virtually every year of our long history—many years with growth of 20 percent or more. Why did I sell? UPI found itself faced with a reality encountered by many companies when they grow to be players in the big leagues. Often they must make greater expenditures and expansions in order to remain competitive. In a dynamic market populated by large, successful, aggressive competitors, a business must grow or it may very well fail.

In order for UPI to remain competitive, annual investments measurable in the millions of dollars loomed on the horizon. These could not with certainty be bankrolled indefinitely, either by our company or by myself personally. Several options were explored, including going public and raising capital through the sale of UPI stock, or attracting a group of investors who would purchase a substantial share of the company. For a combination of reasons, neither of these options was right. I didn't want to be a minority owner or an unheeded voice in my own company. Given the complexity of our business—along with accelerating dependence on new, expensive, and continually changing technologies—I reached a conclusion. The continued growth of UPI and the security of our employees would be more assured if UPI were acquired by a company with greater resources but, at the same time, a similar vision and culture. I began searching for a compatible company.

The search included consideration of thirty-four different companies, not only in the U.S., but also abroad. It led to a firm that had been a tough and respected competitor of ours on many occasions, as both of our firms fought for a larger share of the retirement-services market.

Corporate Courtship

UPI had been courted for more than five years by BISYS Financial Services—a firm that provides many support and outsourcing services for banks and other financial organizations. From time to time, members of the BISYS management team visited us in Brainerd. I accepted their lunch invitations—I hoped to learn more about what they were doing. They were always seeking to acquire UPI. After the dessert course, my answer was always the same: "Thanks, but no thanks."

Once I assessed our future and realized that uniting UPI with another organization was practically inevitable—something I never dreamed I would ever consider—BISYS became the logical choice. Because we had been fierce competitors in providing 401(k) plan services, some in our company seemed to regard BISYS as "the enemy." While that measures their loyalty and their competitive nature, we found no "dark side" to this widely respected company.

Many of the qualities that made us worthy competitors also gave us common ground—a commitment to growth and excellence and a commitment to employees. Though BISYS is a public company, more likely to be driven by bottom-line profitability pressures from stockholders, we believed our union would create a dominant force in the field of retirement services and help ensure a bright future for our employees. Deliberations went on for about two months before the deal was finalized. Among the nonnegotiable elements was my requirement that the buyer must commit to retaining and expanding our Brainerd operation and minimize the loss of positions within these operations.

To make the announcement, we notified each employee in our four Brainerd-area offices that they were to meet at 8 a.m. on Friday, June 1st, 2001, in the Brainerd High School gymnasium—one of the few places in our community large enough to hold our entire staff.

Due to confidentiality rules for companies like BISYS, whose stock is publicly traded, the announcement had to be publicly released in a manner that couldn't be used by anyone for market-trading advantage. The signing of the papers completing the sale had taken place just hours before our employees were informed and BISYS management representatives officially released the news to the financial media.

Mixed Reactions

Our staff had mixed reactions, which could be read on their faces as I stood before them at the podium. I suspect that few had guessed that our firm would be sold. I think the majority expected an announcement of a financing arrangement, a strategic business partnership, or perhaps the sale of part interest in the company to an investor group.

My top management team and I, along with members of the BISYS acquisition team, stressed the compatibility of our companies and the existence of few areas of staff overlap. As a result, a limited number of staff might lose their jobs.

While some later told me they could hardly believe the news, I was heartened tremendously by their immediate reaction. I was given a standing ovation, even though many had to have been wondering whether their jobs might be among those that would be identified as "redundant." The word can be sugarcoated, but there's no sugarcoating its meaning—the loss of one's position—even though the number of positions eliminated was small. Many of these employees were given the option to transfer to another unit within the company. Some, however, due to the uniqueness of their position or combined staffing levels between the two companies, could not remain with the merged UPI-BISYS retirement-services division. These individuals were given severance packages—some very generous considering the length of their service. Others were provided special help because of difficult financial circumstances created by their unexpected job loss. I also made the commitment to divide roughly $1 million among all employees who had been with the company as of January 1st, as thanks for the dedicated service they had given to UPI.

In the days and weeks following the sale, I received dozens of cards, letters, and e-mails from our employees. Without exception, they were appreciative of the opportunity to work under our ownership and leadership. This was even the case with several who lost their positions in the acquisition, yet who still considered their time at UPI to have been rewarding and positive.

Concern Repaid

Many were concerned about how I would handle the loss of my role as leader of UPI. This touched me deeply. People with legitimate concerns for their own welfare, were also concerned about mine. Though I was, and remain, concerned for them, I know that people of this caliber are the kind who will find—or make—opportunities for success. They see the big picture. They are optimists who are concerned for the greater good and the welfare of others. These people are winners. It was rewarding to see how many such people had been part of the UPI team.

Some people, who are more concerned with money than they are with accomplishments, would look at the sum that was paid for UPI—$85 million—and wonder why I would have given a second thought to my departure from the business. Jo Ann and I will never have to worry about financial security for as long as we live.

But money wasn't the main motivator for our accomplishments—it was the many goals that had been set and met. What I miss the most is walking the halls, visiting the various departments, exchanging smiles, shaking hands, and asking—as I did countless times during my twenty-six years of ownership—"Are we winning?" After returning from the Labor Day holiday, I often greeted employees at their desks with, "Happy New Year!" It was like the beginning of a new year to me—the kids were back in school, the summer tourist season was winding down, and it was finally possible to reach someone on the phone! For old time's sake, three months after the sale, I carried on the tradition in September 2001, to boost both my employees' spirits and mine. Before I could say a word, they wished me, "Happy New Year!"

New Horizons

The ink had barely dried on the papers that were signed to change UPI's ownership, when I began thinking about other ventures I might want to pursue. The characteristics that drive a person to build an enterprise, whether as small as a one-person business or as large as UPI, make retirement difficult. The final payoff is not the financial reward. It's envisioning, planning, and executing the dream. Retire? How could a true entrepreneur ever retire?

Epilogue

"Thank you for the opportunity to be part of the UPI vision. Because of you, I have a clear understanding of what 'vision' means . . . You have run a hard, challenging, yet excellent race . . . It's not the money that has made you winners; rather it's the effect you've had on the lives of those around you, the lives that you have touched and blessed."—Susan Larson, executive secretary

"This note is to express my thanks and appreciation . . . you are an entrepreneur in the true sense of the word, and I'm grateful that I had the opportunity to work for you."—Carol Tower

"Through my nine years at UPI, I have stated many times that this is the best company I have ever worked for . . . highly professional, a fair employer, and a fun place to work. These attributes reflect the leadership you have given."—Conith Mackner

"A job well done! . . . I am building my own company now, and hope to use the knowledge and class that you provided in the years we spent together."—Tom Loch, former chief-information officer

"You motivated your people to promote not only their own success, but also the success and reputation of UPI . . . We cared for you and UPI because you cared for all of us, and recognized the contributions we made . . . I am proud to have known and worked for you."—Polly Heins

"Thank you for sharing your infectious enthusiasm and always-positive attitude about overcoming challenges . . . your sense of urgency . . . and—most importantly—for encouraging me to see things that never were and giving me the courage and daring to make them a reality."—Dave Lauer, executive vice-president

"You are certainly the embodiment of the American dream. If you have a vision, are willing to take risks, and work with all your might to realize the vision, the dream will come true. You deserve all the good things that come your way."—Kevin Clark, vice-president and regional sales director

"UPI owes its existence and continuing success to your determination and drive. Your demand for excellence and professsionalism have always set UPI apart . . . This is a great legacy . . . I have always been proud to say I worked for UPI."—Pam O'Rourke, general counsel

"My sincere appreciation for the excitement of being part of a growing company . . . the pride in being part of a great company . . . and learning the true meaning of tenacity. And thank you, also, for your kindness, generosity, and encouragement."—Tom Rutske, human-resources director

"To build a dream—touching the lives of so many people and influencing an entire industry—is something few people will ever experience . . . You and Jo Ann are two of the lucky ones."—Cindy Roggenkamp, vice-president

"You have been a great mentor—teaching me the importance of quality, the excitement of growth, the infectiousness of a positive attitude, and the value of persistence . . . I thank God for having had the honor to work for you, and being able to help create the UPI vision."—Tom Anderson, president